OSPREY
PUBLISHING

US Marine Corps Tank Crewman 1965–70

Vietnam

Ed Gilbert · Illustrated by Howard Gerrard

First published in Great Britain in 2004 by Osprey Publishing, Elms Court, Chapel Way, Botley, Oxford OX2 9LP, United Kingdom.
Email: info@ospreypublishing.com

A CIP catalog record for this book is available from the British Library

ISBN 1 84176 718 2

Ed Gilbert has asserted his right under the Copyright, Designs and Patents Act, 1988, to be identified as the Author of this Work

Editor: Alexander Stilwell
Design: Ken Vail Graphic Design, Cambridge, UK
Index by Glyn Sutcliffe
Originated by Grasmere Digital Imaging, Leeds, UK
Printed in China through World Print Ltd.

04 05 06 07 08   10 9 8 7 6 5 4 3 2 1

FOR A CATALOG OF ALL BOOKS PUBLISHED BY OSPREY MILITARY AND AVIATION PLEASE CONTACT:

The Marketing Manager, Osprey Direct UK, PO Box 140, Wellingborough, Northants, NN8 2FA, United Kingdom.
Email: info@ospreydirect.co.uk

The Marketing Manager, Osprey Direct USA,
c/o MBI Publishing, PO Box 1, 729 Prospect Ave,
Osceola, WI 54020, USA.
Email: info@ospreydirectusa.com

Buy online at **www.ospreypublishing.com**

Artist's note

Readers may care to note that the original paintings from which the color plates in this book were prepared are available for private sale. All reproduction copyright whatsoever is retained by the Publishers. All enquiries should be addressed to:

Howard Gerrard,
11 Oaks Road,
Tenterden,
Kent
TN30 6RD
UK

The Publishers regret that they can enter into no correspondence upon this matter.

Author's Dedication and Acknowledgements

The real war will never get in the books.
                                    Walt Whitman

For Cathy, Jordan, Bill and Jill, and for the late Colonel Thomas A. Simpson (USMCR), Professor and Commanding Officer.

The author is indebted to many individuals, chief among them retired Master Gunnery Sergeant Don Gagnon, editor of the *Marine Corps Tanker's Association Magazine*. Vietnam tankers John Wear, Terry Hunter, Guy Wolfenbarger, Larry Mobley, Jim Carroll (Warrant Officer, USMC ret.), C.C. Casey (Colonel, USMC ret.), and veteran Navy medical corpsman Gene Hackemack patiently answered many questions. I am indebted to Ken Smith-Christmas, Dieter Stenger, Mark Henry and Neil Abelsma of the USMC Museums Branch for their assistance in researching weapons and clothing. All photographs are from the National Archives, the USMC Research Center, the USMC Museums Branch, and the author's collection.

Tank companies in Vietnam were small, tightly knit societies into one of which I have inserted several fictional characters. Of necessity the fictional combats described here are loosely based on actual events. As an example, the incident of the stand-off with enemy sappers atop the tank is based on an actual event that occurred on Goi Noi Island on May 4, 1968, as recounted in Robert E. Peavey's "Scratch My Back", **MCTA Magazine**, December 2000. However, any resemblance of the fictional characters to any persons living or dead is coincidental.

Publisher's Note

Many of the photographs have kindly been provided by either NARA (National Archives and Records Administration) or USMCRC (United States Marine Corps Research Center)

CONTENTS

US MARINE CORPS TANK CREWMAN 1965–70: VIETNAM

INTRODUCTION

The United States Marine Corps has evolved far from its origins as a small shipboard security force, and is unique in its tactical and strategic flexibility. It can deploy a force tailored to fit virtually any mission, whether the requirement be for a small special operations group, a light infantry raiding force, or a division-sized unit complete with tanks, heavy artillery, and fully integrated fixed wing and helicopter air support. Often overlooked in tales of the Corps' many campaigns is the contribution of its tank units.

The most significant step in the evolution of the modern Marine Corps came in 1936 with the formation of the Fleet Marine Force (FMF) divisions, formations designed for amphibious campaigns to secure advanced naval bases in an anticipated war against Japan. It was clear that operations across the vast distances of the Pacific would require each division to be self-sufficient, with its own specialist support units. From its inception, each division included its own tank battalion.

In World War II the divisional tank battalions provided armored firepower in amphibious assaults, protection against enemy armored counter-attacks, and served as assault guns in protracted infantry battles at places like Iwo Jima and Okinawa. The Pacific campaigns also demonstrated the value of tanks in jungle warfare. The tanks further proved themselves in Korea, and by the 1960s were a fundamental part of the Corps' combined arms team.

The Marines routinely deployed tanks with expeditionary units to places like the Lebanon and the Dominican Republic, so when the Marines were ordered to Vietnam in March 1965, they took along their tanks. That decision created a political furor. The presence of the tanks became a lightning rod for accusations of an "escalation" of the war.

The Marine Corps operated in I Corps area, the extreme northern part of the Republic of Vietnam. There they faced not just the indigenous Viet Cong (VC) guerrillas, but conventional units of the North Vietnamese Army (NVA), a highly trained and motivated foe. In the Tet Offensive of early 1968 the VC and NVA seized control of major urban centers, including the cultural and spiritual center of the nation, the ancient capital at Hue.

The recapture of Hue required the Marines to reorient themselves from rural anti-guerrilla operations to conventional combat in an urban setting. The ability to undertake such a radical change within days, and to prevail against superior numbers in savage urban combat, demonstrated the versatility, courage, and tenacity that are the hallmarks of the "ordinary" Marine.

This narrative covers the combat experiences of three fictional

Marine tankers – Carlos Entenza, Parker Butler, and Nicholas Berwick –

during the period immediately prior to and during the Tet Offensive, and the pivotal battle for Hue City. The minor character Knowles is also fictional. Additional characters such as Colonel "Case" Casey, Master Gunnery Sergeant Don Gagnon, and Warrant Officer Jim Carroll are actual persons who served in Marine Corps tank units in Vietnam.

CHRONOLOGY

1954
October: Following a disastrous defeat at Din Bien Phu in May, French colonial troops depart. Vietnam is partitioned into the Communist Peoples' Republic of Vietnam (PRVN) and the non-Communist Republic of Vietnam (RVN).

1957
After consolidating power in the north, Communist forces commence a guerrilla war against the RVN.

1961
US supplies direct military aid to the RVN in response to increased Communist subversion.

1964
US warships are attacked in the Gulf of Tonkin. President Lyndon Johnson gains Congressional approval for military intervention, the Tonkin Gulf Resolution.

1965
US aircraft support facilities in northern RVN attacked. US tactical bombing of the PRVN commences. United States Marines are committed to provide protection for American ground installations. The 3d Platoon, B Company, 3d Marine Tank Battalion is the first American armored unit committed to the war.

1966
Strategic bombing of North Vietnam commences. US ground forces escalate, including establishment of major USMC bases at Chu Lai and Danang.

1967
US forces are engaged in increasingly heavy combat throughout RVN. The Marines deploy northward to defend the Demilitarized Zone that divides the two Vietnams.

1968
This will prove to be the bloodiest year of the Vietnam War.
January–April: Marines are besieged at the Khe Sanh forward combat base near the Laotian border. The Tet (Lunar New Year) Communist offensive results in heavy urban combat, particularly in parts of Saigon and Hue.
March–May: The US bombing offensive against the North is scaled back in response to negotiation offers.
November: Richard Nixon elected president with a "secret plan to end the war".

1969
January: Truce negotiations begin in Paris.
July: Withdrawal of US troops begins.

1970
March: US and RVN forces invade Cambodia, triggering massive anti-war protests in the US.
July: American forces are withdrawn from Cambodia.

Vietnamese women bearing flower garlands provided an incongruous greeting for the amphibious landing of the first American tanks in Vietnam, from the 3d Tank Battalion, 9th Marine Expeditionary Brigade. (NARA)

December: US Congress repeals the Tonkin Gulf Resolution that provided authorization for the undeclared war.

1971
February: RVN troops invade Laos.
July: Last USMC combat units depart RVN.

1972
March: North Vietnam invades RVN with conventional forces, triggering a resumption of US bombing against the North. Marine Corps advisors to RVN Marine Corps are engaged in combat.
May: North Vietnamese ports are mined and bombing escalates.
August: Last US ground combat forces depart RVN, but logistical personnel, advisors and other support personnel remain.

1973
January: Peace agreement between US and North Vietnam.
March: Last US forces depart RVN.

1975
NVA forces complete logistical build-up on RVN territory, including airfield complexes, roads, and pipelines.
March: Major invasion by conventional forces of the NVA commences.
30 April: NVA tanks crash through the gates of the RVN Presidential Palace in Saigon. The war is over.

ENLISTMENT

There were as many reasons for enlisting in the Marine Corps as there were individual Marines. The Corps has always prided itself upon being a volunteer organization, and through most of its history has not accepted conscripts. The two exceptions have occurred when rapid expansion created manpower needs that outstripped the ability to attract volunteers. In 1967 the Vietnam conflict required the Corps to accept draftees (conscripts), and during the course of the war some 19,000 conscripts served in the Marine Corps. To compound recruiting problems, Secretary of Defense Robert S. McNamara instituted Project 100,000. This program forced the Corps to accept 18 percent of its new recruits from a pool of men who had previously been considered mentally unsuited for military service, actually reducing available openings for more qualified recruits.

Male Americans were (and still are) required to register with the Selective Service Administration within ninety days of reaching their eighteenth birthday. In the late 1960s registrants were assigned a draft number, and a classification. Classifications ranged from 4-F (completely unqualified for military service because of physical or mental infirmity), through 1-Y (suited for service only in time of national emergency), to 1-A (suited for immediate service). Other temporary classifications could defer military service for a variety of reasons – most typically, to study at a university (2-S), to provide support for children or disabled parents, or to serve in a critical industry such as farming. A local draft board made up of political appointees reviewed each individual's classification.

Each region of the country was required to supply a quota of young men, and there was considerable pressure to classify as many as possible 1-A. One side effect of the draft was to limit employment options for young men as employers were reluctant to hire and train employees who would soon disappear into the military. Although the draft and military service would become increasingly unpopular as the war dragged on, in the early years of the conflict there was a strong desire to both serve the nation and to combat Communism. Other young men had grown up in families with a strong military tradition, with fathers and uncles who recounted tales – usually romanticized and stripped of the horrors they had experienced – of their service in World War II and Korea. For others the motivation was a diet of films and television shows depicting an even more romanticized version of war.

Regardless of motivation, many young men chose to "beat the draft" by voluntary enlistment in a particular branch of

Map of the I Corps Military Region, the five northern provinces of South Vietnam, with sites mentioned in the text.

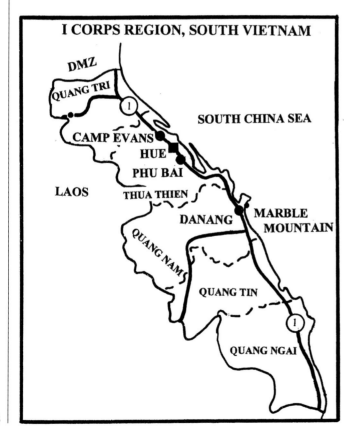

military service. For the more adventurous, and certainly for many young men who for one reason or another wished to test their own mettle, the Marine Corps was the preferred branch of service.

The Marine Corps attracted the adventurous because it had long been one of the most astute users of advertising to promote its interests, including recruiting. The classic Marine Corps recruiting slogan, "The Marine Corps Builds Men", was designed to challenge the young male. The Corps also made skillful use of Hollywood, providing both technical advice and active cooperation. Many of these joint products have become classic war movies. *The Sands of Iwo Jima* starring John Wayne incorporated combat film footage (including some of the author's uncle) from the savage battles for Tarawa and Iwo Jima. Jack Webb played the title role in *The DI*, one of the very few films to concentrate upon the training and indoctrination process for any service or country. Although real Marines knew that it glossed over the harsh and sometimes outright brutal recruit training of the era, it was a wildly popular film. Perhaps the most complete cooperation came with the filming of *The Halls of Montezuma*, a fictional rendering of the experiences of Marines in the Marianas campaigns of mid-1944, starring Richard Widmark. The elaborate battle scenes were staged at Camp Pendleton, California, in early 1950. The vast majority of the "extras" were not actors but Marine infantrymen of the 5th Marines (a rifle regiment) and the 1st Marine Tank Battalion, who would within months be dispatched to South Korea to counter a North Korean invasion.

Parker Butler was a typical young recruit. A native of central Mississippi, in May 1965 he was experiencing his final weeks of high school (secondary school). Locked in an ongoing adolescent struggle with his tyrannical stepfather, and with limited job prospects, Parker angrily decided to enlist in the service as a way out of a stifling small-town life. As usual, both the Navy and the Air Force recruiters described the educational and world-travel advantages of their service in glowing terms. Both were eager to accept him, but said that he would have to delay his departure for several months.

In contrast, Marine Corps recruiters often applied "reverse psychology" because they considered themselves representatives of an elite service.

The Marine recruiting sergeant was a weathered middle-aged man with short-cropped hair, immaculately attired in dress-blue trousers with a wide red stripe down each leg, and a sharply creased tan shirt marked by rows of brightly colored campaign ribbons. Rather than launching into a discussion about what his service could offer in the way of careers and job training, the grim old sergeant simply asked Parker why the Corps should even want him.

In response to Parker's stumbling reply, the man explained that to become a Marine had to be earned, sometimes at a very high price. The question was not one of if the service was good enough for Parker, but

American males over the age of 18 were required to carry an identification card and a draft status card at all times. At the time this card was issued, the author was a part-time university student and not eligible for the 2-S student deferment. (Author)

whether he was good enough to be a Marine. Parker got his first lesson in the history and traditions – sometimes highly romanticized – that drive the Corps and its mythology.

"Son, do you see this red stripe on my trousers? In the battle for Chepultepec in 1846, all the officers and sergeants were killed or wounded, but their Marines went on to capture the Halls of Montezuma. If you're a leader, you can wear this stripe. But more important, it reminds all Marines that every one of them privates knew what he had to do, without being led. You think you got that in you?"

With his male pride challenged, Parker was not about to back down. "When can I go?" he asked the sergeant.

The recruiting sergeant explained that if he could pass the rigorous physical examination and graduate from high school, he could depart for boot camp – as the basic training for Marines is called – within weeks.

The thorough physical and dental examination, administered by a Navy medical officer in a nearby city (medical, dental, and chaplain services for the Marine Corps are provided by the Navy), determined that Parker was slightly under the desired weight for his height, but otherwise suited for the rigors of recruit training. In the later years of the Vietnam conflict, as manpower requirements soared, the strict physical requirements would be somewhat relaxed. With the black humor typical of Marines, one popular joke held that the physical consisted of a checklist: "Arms – two, legs – two, head – one, lungs – at least one. Congratulations, you passed." Of course, standards were never actually that low – indeed, in 1965 the Corps could still afford to accept only the very best physical and mental specimens.

When Parker boarded the bus for recruit training at Parris Island, South Carolina, both sides were winners. The Corps had a new recruit, and Parker was on his way to test himself in one of the most rigorous schools his nation had to offer.

Carlos Entenza grew up in what was at that time still a rather sheltered Hispanic community in San Antonio, Texas, and graduated from high school in 1966. Highly motivated and intelligent, Carlos lacked both the educational preparation and the financial resources to attend college. Although not yet hard pressed by the draft, he found himself trapped in a series of low-paying jobs with little or no chance of advancement.

The training and discipline offered by the Corps, and the GI Bill, which paid an educational stipend to veterans, were powerful incentives for Carlos. Like many young working-class men of his generation, a stronger motivation was to prove himself within his family. His father and uncles still held a fond view of their Marine Corps service in the Pacific War and Korea. As young men they had been given the opportunity to demonstrate their masculine prowess in an environment relatively free of the prejudice often experienced by Mexican-Americans at home in Texas.

The uncles gladly gave Carlos a realistic assessment of what awaited him. Each of them regaled him with tales of the harshness and physical torment of boot camp. One uncle, more astute than the others, dispassionately described how the whole purpose was to break him down, distill away his soft civilian attitudes, and harden him into the type of man who is prepared, both physically and mentally, to undertake seemingly impossible tasks. He went on to describe the drill instructors as the best practical psychologists in the world, who used psychological conditioning techniques based on decades of experience, rather than on academic theories. He said that even if you knew what was happening, you would be powerless to resist. Better men than Carlos had tried.

Of course the dark side to the intense training was that some men broke under the strain. The mental toughening process sought to identify those men who were not likely to successfully endure the stress of combat.

Comparing these descriptions to those of his high-school friends who had already enlisted or been drafted into other services simply steeled Carlos's resolve. He had already adopted the "If you're going to fight, fight alongside the best" attitude shared by many young Marines of the period. The psychological conditioning that is a fundamental part of each Marine's training had already begun.

TRAINING

Parker Butler enlisted with no clear idea of the career path he wanted to take. He found that the highly organized structure of military life suited him, and that the rules – while sometimes harsh and restrictive – were not as arbitrary as those imposed by his stepfather. Originally assigned to the infantry, he volunteered to extend his enlistment in order to transfer to the 2d Tank Battalion at Camp Lejeune, North Carolina.

Most of Parker's training in the tank battalion was what the Marines called OJT – On the Job Training. He observed others in performance of various tasks, and then imitated them. This type of specialist training was once common, but was unusual by the 1960s. As a new man and a "dumb ol' grunt" (infantryman) he was subjected to the usual forms of harassment, such as being sent to the maintenance shop to ask for a "road wheel pump" for the solid rubber wheels, a specialized left-handed wrench, and other non existent items.

An important aspect of this training was rotation through all the crew positions, from the lowliest – loader for the main gun – through gunner, driver, and tank commander. A quick learner, Parker rose rapidly to the rank of Sergeant. He eventually received orders to take a two-week Christmas leave, and report for service in Vietnam in early 1968.

Boot camp

Carlos Entenza's experience was more typical. He was among the last recruits of the Vietnam generation to receive the full benefit of lengthy "peacetime training". Since his home was west of the Mississippi River, Carlos should have been a "Hollywood Marine", trained at the Marine Corps Recruit Depot (MCRD) at San Diego, California. However, fate, in the form of the Corps' scheduling requirements, intervened and Carlos went by commercial airline to Savannah, Georgia.

The bus from the airport arrived aboard MCRD Parris Island, South Carolina, at 2.00 am in gentle, steaming rain. Carlos and thirty others tumbled out of the bus following the instructions of a bass voice that left absolutely no doubt that they were now the lowest possible form of life – a Marine Corps "boot", or trainee. Under the lash of creative

Drill instructors harass a new recruit at the Marine Corps Recruit Depot, Parris Island, South Carolina. The "boot" wears the silver-painted "chrome dome" helmet liner, and carries all his new belongings in a seabag. (NARA)

profanities and insults bellowed by drill instructors clad in immaculately tailored uniforms and the famous "Smoky Bear" campaign hats, the herd of civilians arranged themselves on yellow footprints painted onto the surface of the parking lot. This was their introduction to the one proper way to perform any specific task, beginning with arranging themselves in precisely aligned rows and standing at attention with heels together and feet apart at a precise 45-degree angle.

Once inside the Receiving Barracks, each recruit's individuality was systematically dismantled. Hair was shorn close to the scalp in a six-second haircut, for which their pay was docked twenty-five cents. Personal belongings were packed into a paper bag for later return. A variety of contraband, from switchblade knives to condoms brought aboard by the more ill informed or optimistic, was discarded in the trash.

In a disorienting blur of straggling marches and long queues the boots acquired the necessities of their new life. Clothing, personal items, cleaning equipment, web gear (called "782 gear" by the Marines, after the numbered form the Marine signs when it is issued to him) went into his "luggage" – a capacious green seabag (duffel) and a steel bucket.

Early on the sleep-deprived boots were given a series of mental aptitude tests. Carlos struggled to remain awake in the stagnant air of a closed room sweltering in the South Carolina heat. Huge sweat drops spotted the machine-graded forms on which the recruits answered the questions. None realized that the answers they gave to the strange questions would help determine their Military Occupational Specialty, or MOS.

The recruits began to learn a new vocabulary. Reflecting its origins as a shipboard service, the Corps utilizes its own language in which floors are "decks", the drinking fountain (and the rumors exchanged there) are the "scuttlebutt", and one attends to bodily functions at a "head call". An affirmative answer might be either "yes" (statement of a fact) or "aye-aye" ("I hear and will obey").

The boot's basic wardrobe consisted of baggy green utility trousers ("Girls wear pants, idiot!"), white boxer shorts and T-shirt (called "skivvies"), sturdy box-toed leather combat boots, and the "chrome dome", a plastic helmet liner painted silver to reflect the brutal heat of the South Carolina sun.

Despite the seeming harshness, rigid rules governed the treatment of recruits. In 1956 six recruits drowned in the "Ribbon Creek Massacre", an ill-advised disciplinary night march through the Carolina swamps. The resulting reforms guaranteed eight hours sleep per night (unless the recruit had some form of internal security watch), suspension of training under extreme heat conditions, and limitations upon physical punishment.

Carlos was overweight, but more importantly he was unable to achieve an acceptable score on the first Physical Readiness Test (PRT), a timed combination of push-ups, pull-ups, sit-ups, a 3-mile (5-km) run, and other exercises. He was assigned to the "fatbody platoon" of the Special Training Branch, where the regime was a strict diet and eight hours a day of intense exercise until he could both reach an acceptable weight and pass the PRT. The corresponding group was the "skinnybody platoon", whose residents were required to consume twice the normal amount of food as well as pass the PRT. Graduates were then returned to the normal training cycle.

The remainder of boot camp systematically dismantled Carlos's civilian attitudes and transformed him into a basic Marine. More important than his greatly improved physical condition and swimming ability, familiarity with naval jargon, and proficiency with the rifle, bayonet, and in unarmed combat, was a new creed. When ordered to do the impossible, the only acceptable answer was "Aye aye, sir." The Roman Catholic Carlos learned there was now an eighth deadly sin – to fail the Corps or his comrades.

Like the other recruits, Carlos accepted the Drill Instructor's indoctrination that the infantryman was the purest form of Marine. Carlos wanted to be a "grunt", and was bitterly disappointed to be assigned an MOS of 1811 – basic tank crewman – rather than the infantry. Some recruits cried when assigned to a non-combat MOS.

Infantry Training Regiment

The 1st Infantry Training Regiment (ITR) at Camp Lejeune, North Carolina, further refined Carlos's military skills, and provided a taste of the brutal life of the infantrymen he was pledged to support. ITR developed a basic proficiency with every weapon in the Marine Corps inventory, from pistols to flamethrowers, as well as skills like small unit tactics, night combat, map reading and compass navigation, escape and evasion, scouting and reporting, and living out of a backpack. The men were now full-fledged Marines, and the protective regulations that had governed life in boot camp no longer applied. To better simulate the rigors of combat, training continued around the clock. Trainees were fortunate to get four hours sleep each night, two if assigned to guard duty, patrolling, or another activity, so they learned to fight fatigue with brief catnaps.

Tank school

After completion of ITR and promotion to Private First Class (PFC), Carlos reported to the Basic Armored Vehicle Crewman's School at Camp Del Mar, a part of the sprawling base at Camp Pendleton, California, where the technical training provided was far more individualized. The forty-eight students in Carlos's class lived in a central school barracks under the care and supervision of a non-commissioned officer (NCO – Corporal and above) troop handler who was responsible for discipline, clothing, and the general welfare of the students. For instructional purposes trainees were placed under the supervision of experienced instructors who would shepherd them through their training.

About two-thirds of the instruction was classroom work, learning technical specifications, maintenance procedures, and other basic

RIGHT **The man at left tosses a practice grenade through a doorway as Marines in the 1st Infantry Training Regiment practice urban combat. Such training proved to be valuable in the battle for Hue in February 1968. (NARA)**

BELOW **A Private First Class in the tank school at Camp Pendleton, California checks track connector bolts. Routine maintenance tasks were a major part of the tanker's training. (NARA)**

information. Much of Carlos's life would henceforth be governed by the knowledge contained in "Operator's Manual, Tank, Combat, Full Tracked, 90mm Gun, M48A3 W/E", a hefty loose-leaf volume with yellow paper covers, bound together by three aluminum screws.

Because tanks are expensive to operate and require the constant attentions of maintenance personnel, the military developed simulators upon which the students could learn the basics of operating the tank. The driver simulator allowed the student to familiarize himself with the tank's controls. Students could also practice gunnery and turret drill in a turret mounted on a stationary stand.

After familiarization the student crews were placed under the supervision of an experienced NCO tank commander and driving instructor, and allowed inside a real tank. After a period of observation inside the moving tank, the students were allowed to drive along the beach near Camp Del Mar, and eventually along the unpaved roads and on to the training ranges near Interstate Highway Five. This period of training lasted about five days.

The students were also responsible for general maintenance of their vehicle. "At-a-halt" checks were performed each time the tank stopped for any period of time. The students scurried to check engine oil, fluid levels, and cable connections for the six heavy batteries, track tension, track end-connectors, road wheel bolts, and felt each road wheel bearing to check for overheating. At the end of the day the students were responsible for more cleaning, suspension lubrication, and adjusting the track tension under the supervision of the instructor. An unlucky few had the experience of reversing the sprockets, a twice-yearly task that consisted of pulling off the tracks, removing the rear drive sprockets and exchanging the right and left sprockets to compensate for uneven wear.

This phase of training also included subjects that could only be simulated on a real tank: use of the escape hatch in the floor of the tank, and evacuation of wounded crewmen. They also learned the valuable lesson that sometimes age and experience count for more than youthful agility and exuberance. One day Master Sergeant Don Gagnon, the senior instructor in the tank school, watched as a group of students bet twenty dollars that one of the instructors – who weighed nearly 200lb (91kg) but stood only 5ft 7in. (170cm) tall – could not go in through the tank commander's hatch, down through the turret and out through the tiny escape hatch in under twenty seconds. The students lost the bet to the veteran tanker.

Trainees use pinch bars to align a broken track at the Camp Pendleton tank school. The red warning flag on the tank commander's cupola indicates that the tank is immobilized in the road, and is a crash hazard. (NARA)

Experienced instructors like Gagnon thought that there was never enough actual hands-on experience with the tanks. Each student received about five days' driving experience and two days at the gunnery range where each man loaded and fired five rounds from the 90mm main gun; they also fired the .30-cal. coaxial machine gun and the tank commander's .50-cal. machine gun.

The students did not receive any hands-on experience with either M67 flame tanks, externally identical to the M48A3 gun tank, or the M103A2 heavy tanks with their huge 120mm guns, although they were allowed to chamber a wooden practice round inside the M103A2, and watched live-fire demonstrations of both vehicles on the range. Training for service in these specialized vehicles was conducted within the active tank battalions. (The flame tanks were in the Headquarters Company of each Tank Battalion. The M103A2s made up a separate heavy tank company in each battalion, but were not used in Vietnam.)

Upon graduation, Carlos was assigned to the 5th Tank Battalion at Camp Pendleton. Despite good evaluations in tank school, Carlos discovered that his position in the new unit depended not upon proficiency, but chance. A new man was incorporated where he was needed, usually as a loader. A lucky few started as tank commanders. In training, however, each man periodically assumed each of the other crew positions in order to maintain his overall proficiency.

For months his life in the unit was easy and uneventful. Working days consisted of routine maintenance of both the tanks and the physical facilities of the base. On weekend liberties the young Marines went into the adjacent town of Oceanside, ventured farther afield to San Diego or Los Angeles, and sampled the riskier nightlife of Tijuana, just across the border into Mexico. But all the young Marines knew that, barring some administrative oversight, all were just biding their time before a trip to Vietnam. Carlos's turn came in mid-1967.

BELIEF AND BELONGING

Like other military organizations with a long tradition of service, the United States Marine Corps places great emphasis upon its history and traditions. While the technical aspects of the weapons used by Marines have changed over the decades, the training used to instill personal and unit pride has changed little since World War II. This pride served the Corps well during the Vietnam era, helping to maintain morale even as the war became increasingly controversial.

Then as now a great deal of each Marine's training, from boot camp through specialist training, was carefully crafted to instill a powerful sense of pride in himself and the Corps. Marines were required to maintain a high level of physical strength and agility, but when a man is called upon to perform beyond any reasonable human expectation, the will is more important than the body. Marines called this sense of mission and the expectation of high individual and collective performance *esprit de corps*. It rested upon a powerful tripod of history and unit pride, individual pride, and peer pressure.

For the recruit who enlisted in the 1967–68 period, the Marine Corps' reputation as an elite force was forged in terrible combat from Belleau Wood in 1918 to the jungles of Vietnam. Each of these battles was fought by very ordinary men called upon to do extraordinary deeds, and so from his first day each Marine was reminded of the achievements of those who had gone before him. Mottoes and quotations were stenciled onto the bulkheads of the receiving barracks where he began his training. He was trained in "History and Traditions", and tested for proficiency in that area just as in fieldcraft or rifle marksmanship.

In addition to tales of legendary victories like Iwo Jima and Belleau Wood, recruits learned of the small garrison on Wake Island. In 1942 they held out for weeks against the Japanese before being overwhelmed by vastly superior numbers. The heroism of the doomed garrison provided a much-needed boost to national morale in the darkest days of the war.

In December 1950, the 1st Marine Division found itself surrounded by seven Chinese Communist divisions in the mountains of northern Korea. While the world awaited its destruction, the division fought its way out, bringing its wounded and dead, and savaging the Chinese divisions. Their march to the sea saved the entire United Nations X Corps from annihilation.

Recruits learned about individual role models, chief among them Lewis Burwell Puller, or "Chesty", who rose from private to Lieutenant General and fought in the "Banana Wars" of the 1920s, in the savage battles against Japan, and again in Korea. In northern Korea Puller's regiment was surrounded, fighting desperately against two Chinese divisions to hold open the route of the retreat for the 1st Marine Division. His comment on the situation is still a Marine Corps classic: "We've been looking for the enemy for several days now. We've finally found them. We're surrounded. That simplifies our problem of getting to these people and killing them." Other heroes included Sergeant Major Dan Daly, holder of two Medals of Honor, and Sergeant John Basilone, a machine gunner who almost single-handedly fought off a Japanese regiment on Guadalcanal.

The purpose of this historical indoctrination was to instill a sense of unit pride, and to provide role models for young Marines.

The physical and mental severity of boot camp also forged a common bond among those who experienced it, and imparted a powerful sense of pride in self. The individual knew that he had survived one of the harshest experiences American society could legally provide. Three decades later the former Marine often has a complex love-hate relationship with the Corps, resenting the harshness while realizing that the experience imparted confidence that he could endure, survive, and prevail against almost any problem life might present.

The determination not to fail was above all expressed in a man's dedication to his fellow Marines. Long before it was common among Special Forces, the credo of recovering their dead brethren was an article of faith among Marines. In 1950, North Korean prisoners under interrogation often remarked that they did not like to fight "the men with yellow legs [referring to the distinctive canvas gaiters then worn by Marines] who always want their dead men back."

Sergeant David J. Danner exhibited this dedication to other Marines in Vietnam. He was awarded the Navy Cross, the Marine Corps' second highest award for bravery.

His citation reads:

For extraordinary heroism as a Tank Maintenance Man and Crewman with Company A, Third Tank Battalion, Third Marine Division, in connection with operations against the enemy in the Republic of Vietnam on 8 May 1967. While operating in support of the First Battalion, Fourth Marines, Sergeant Danner's tank was hit and heavily damaged by enemy fire during a savage mortar and infantry attack on the battalion's positions at Gio Linh by a 400-man North Vietnamese Army force. Although wounded himself, Sergeant Danner helped his dazed and wounded fellow crewmen from the tank to the medical aid station. Realizing that enemy soldiers were in the Command Post area, having penetrated the defensive perimeter during their initial assault, he refused first aid and resolutely returned to his disabled tank to retrieve a .30-caliber machine gun. Mounting the weapon on the ground, he commenced delivering a heavy volume of fire on the attackers. With complete disregard for his own safety, he repeatedly left his position to deliver badly needed ammunition to the infantrymen in the fighting holes and to assist in moving casualties to safer positions. On one occasion, observing a seriously wounded Marine in need of immediate medical treatment, Sergeant Danner carried the man through intense enemy fire to the corpsman's bunker where he could receive life-saving first aid, which prevented him from bleeding to death. Demonstrating uncommon courage and tenacity, he then returned to his machine gun where he continued to provide covering fire for his comrades, moving his weapon to alternate positions in order to deliver maximum fire on the enemy. Although in extreme pain from fragment wounds to his arms and back and suffering from severe burns and a loss of hearing as a result of an explosion, he selflessly disregarded his own welfare throughout the vicious firefight in order to assist his comrades in repulsing the North Vietnamese attack. By his exceptional professional skill and bold initiative, he personally killed fifteen enemy soldiers and undoubtedly wounded many more. Sergeant Danner's daring and heroic actions at great personal risk, inspiring leadership, and unwavering devotion to duty reflected great credit upon himself and were in keeping with the highest traditions of the Marine Corps and the United States Naval Service.

APPEARANCE AND DRESS

Until the early days of World War II, the Marine's everyday and combat uniforms were the same; web gear and helmet were simply added to the everyday uniform. The first utilities were issued as work uniforms to prevent dirtying the everyday uniform. During World War II these evolved into the standard combat uniform of Marines.

The boot was issued several sets of "skivvies", white cotton boxer-style undershorts and T-shirts. The recruits then passed along one side of a

Mail was extremely important to maintain morale, and considerable effort was expended to pick up and deliver mail even when a unit was in combat. This Marine is using a ration box as a writing desk. Note the P-38 can opener on the box. (USMCRC)

wooden counter to receive two sets of utilities – trousers, shirts (called jackets by the Marines) and caps (called covers). Junior supply men made a cursory attempt to measure sizes, but often simply guessed at the correct size. If the fit were outrageously poor, the items would be replaced, at the discretion of the Drill Instructor. The new recruit's uniform was not ironed, and the rumpled appearance was part of the psychological reduction process.

Basic service uniforms

The M62 Utility Uniform was sage green cotton sateen (a closely woven cotton fabric that had a glossy surface when new) with plastic buttons. The fabric did not "breathe" well to shed water vapor, and was extremely unpleasant to wear in the subtropical summer of South Carolina. All closures were provided with buttons for ease of repair, and all buttons except the topmost collar button were to be worn fastened at all times. Jackets were long sleeved, and in hot weather (defined by calendar date, not temperature) the sleeves were rolled above the elbow.

The most distinctive features of this uniform were the cover and the trouser belt. The kepi-style cover was worn blocked and starched in a multi-sided shape unlike the cylindrical and later baseball-style caps issued to the Army. The belt buckle was an open frame design, unlike the Army's solid brass panel design.

Other issue clothing included athletic clothing, canvas basketball shoes for physical training, and a few other miscellaneous items. One of the recruit's first responsibilities was to stamp his name on most items using a stamping kit provided as part of his Post Exchange (PX) gear. (This item, along with a razor and shaving supplies, dental hygiene products, metal and shoe polish, and other personal items were provided as a package, with the cost deducted from the boot's pay.)

New recruits were not issued dress clothing. Unlike today, the utility uniform was never worn off the base, even for travel to personal housing, a rule rigidly enforced by the Military Police. Any recruit who chose to absent himself would be obvious to the general population surrounding the base, many of them retired military men.

Considerable care was exercised to provide the correct fit for footgear. Until 1969 the standard combat boot was a heavy, solid leather boot with eighteen eyelets and a sturdy replaceable sole and heel. Carlos's Senior Drill Instructor was an old infantryman who took the welfare of his men's feet very seriously. He had his recruits "break in" their boots by wearing them into the shower until they were thoroughly soaked, and then wearing them – including sleeping in them – until

This "official portrait" of the M62 utility uniform, worn with the heavy leather combat boots, depicts the proper positioning of all markings and rank badges, and the proper length of the web trouser belt. (NARA)

they dried. This molded the leather to the shape of the foot, preventing many a blister in later service. These boots were without doubt the most durable item of the Marine's gear, and the author's are still serviceable thirty years later.

An inexpensive boot with an integral rubber sole (sometimes called the "McNamara boot" after then Secretary of Defense, Robert S. McNamara) later replaced the sturdy leather boot. When the sole of the "McNamara boot" wore out, the whole boot was discarded.

In the last phases of training the recruits starched and ironed their utilities daily as a sign of higher status. This task, along with polishing boots and brass, mending tears and other sewing, washing clothing by hand, taking a shower, and all personal tasks such as writing letters, were completed during the boot's one hour of nightly "free time". Thus each Marine learned how to care for both himself and his clothing quickly and efficiently.

In the early phase of training boots wore the utility trousers rolled into an untidy cuff at the ankle. In the final phase of training, recruits were allowed to blouse their trouser legs. Unlike the Army, who tucked the trouser leg into the boot top, Marines rolled the trouser leg outside in and secured it with a blousing garter, a long coiled spring with hooks on the end.

Another ego boost for final-phase recruits was longer hair to distinguish them from the shaven-headed early-phase recruits. The hair on the top of the head was allowed to grow out to about an inch/2.5cm in length. Facial hair was shaven each day, with sideburns no lower than the hole in the ear. The more hirsute were required to shave as far down as the neckline of the skivvie shirt.

In the final phase of training the boot was issued a custom tailored set of dress uniforms. These consisted of leather oxford shoes (kept polished to a mirror gloss), nylon dress socks, winter and summer uniforms including the field scarf (necktie) and dress covers, a nylon raincoat, and such details as collar stays and a tie clasp. The famous dress-blue uniform was issued only to the outstanding recruit in each training platoon, and to personnel whose duties might require it.

Once on active duty the individual Marine was expected to keep his uniforms neat and in good repair at all times. This included careful application of the iron-on transfer of the eagle-globe-and-anchor symbol and the letters USMC on the breast pocket of the utility jacket, with a smaller symbol on the front of the cover. The hair could be worn somewhat longer, but no more than 3in./7.5cm on the top, tapering to zero at the natural hairline. Moustaches could be worn, but in practice were usually limited to officers or NCOs. Such a moustache could extend no farther down than the top edge of the lip, and no farther to the sides than the corners of the mouth.

Tracked vehicle crew uniforms

Men who worked as mechanics on tanks, artillery pieces, and motor vehicles were issued a sage-green, one-piece coverall. It was strictly a work uniform, and was not worn outside of repair shops.

Crewmen on tanks, amphibian tractors, and the small "Ontos" tank destroyer, as well as the drivers and vehicle commanders of self-propelled artillery pieces, wore a one-piece plastic crash helmet designed to protect the head from injuries caused by the head smashing against interior surfaces. This consisted of a shell that cradled the skull and ears, with an internal web suspension system. Earphones and a microphone mounted on a wire frame at the front were connected to a cable that clipped to the rear of the helmet, to keep it out of the way in the confines of the tank. This cable connected to the tank's intercom system, allowing the crew to communicate over the roar of the engine, the squealing tracks, and the noise of the guns.

The crewman's helmet was painted dark Forest Green with a granular surface, and had black plastic trim and brown electrical component housings. In some units a unit marking or tank number might be applied to the back of the helmet. The crew helmet provided no protection against bullets or shrapnel.

Uniforms in Vietnam

The first Marines deployed to Vietnam wore the M62 utility uniforms and leather combat boots, but these quickly proved impractical in the climate. By 1967 Army-style "jungle utilities" were in common but by no means universal use. These were made of a fabric that would allow more efficient evaporation of perspiration, and had far more pocket space to allow men to carry various items in more convenient spots than in the backpack. Camouflage pattern jungle utilities appeared during mid-1968.

The jungle utility jacket had four pockets, including two waist pockets, which meant that the shirt tail had to be worn outside the trousers. The two breast pockets were sewn on a diagonal, to make them easier to reach into with the opposite hand, but this meant that the treasured "bird-on-a-ball" symbol could not be worn on the pocket.

The trousers had spacious bellows pockets on the outside of each leg. For a tanker who had to move around inside a cramped vehicle as well as through narrow hatches, these pockets were more of a liability.

Another new item was the tropical sun hat, a wide-brimmed soft hat made of the same material as the utility uniform. The "boonie hat" provided more protection from the sun, and could be easily wadded up and stored in a pocket when not in use. Most of these hats were locally made in Vietnam, and varied considerably in design.

The most distinctive clothing item of the Vietnam War was the jungle boot. The leather combat boot and its inexpensive replacement were both ill suited to the tropical environment of Vietnam – once soaked, both types of boot took days to dry, and for infantrymen wading through

This tank sergeant in Vietnam wears the jungle utility jacket with M62 trousers. Note the absence of an undershirt and the loosely laced boots on the man in the background. The sergeant is holding part of a wheel assembly blown off by the explosion of a mine. (USMCRC)

streams and flooded rice paddies this meant that the boots stayed permanently wet. It might be a race to determine which rotted first, the boots or the wearer's feet.

The jungle boot was made with a combination black leather and green nylon fabric upper, glued to a thick rubber sole with a heavy tread. The uppers had two small brass drain meshes built into the inside arch to allow excess water to drain out, and additional water could evaporate through the fabric. The feet of men wearing these boots might never truly dry out, but at least they did not remain completely sodden.

The thick sole incorporated metal plates to help reduce injuries caused by punji stakes – sharpened sticks, often covered with human feces – used as a booby trap by the Viet Cong. The major disadvantage of this boot was the lug sole. Glutinous clay-rich mud clung to the lugs, converting each foot into a ball of mud that hobbled the wearer. A design introduced later in the war featured a simplified sole that to some extent remedied this problem.

Despite America's wealth and a well-developed logistical support system, none of these specialized uniform items were universally available in 1967–68. Jungle utilities were issued in limited quantities, and infantry units had first call on available supplies. Marines wore one or both styles, and mixing the jacket from one type with the trousers from the other was common. A mix of utility covers and boonie hats were worn with this grab bag of uniforms.

Many tankers wore the standard combat boot in Vietnam. The heavy boot provided better foot protection for men working with heavy tools and machinery. Later in the war the jungle boot became the standard footwear for tankers, too.

The M51 or M55 protective vest was issued to all Marines in Vietnam. The bulky appearance imparted by internal metal plates distinguishes these vests from the later models worn by Army troops. The armored vest was not bulletproof, but provided protection against low-velocity fragmentation such as grenade splinters and some artillery shrapnel.

Marines around a damaged tank exhibit a mixture of uniforms. The man at left wears M62 trousers and the jungle utility jacket. The man with the carbine is wearing an M62 jacket with the jungle trousers. (USMCRC)

The vest came in two models, with either two or four pockets on the front. It could be closed at the front by a heavy zipper and snaps, but was usually worn open. A suspension system at the lower edge allowed various items to be carried attached to the vest, and it had a raised ridge stitched onto the right shoulder to make carrying a slung rifle easier.

Tank crewmen often wore the flak vest outside the tank, but the cramped confines and heat made it impractical to wear it while inside. It was more common for the tank commander to wear the vest, since he often rode exposed atop his cupola in order to have a better view of the battlefield.

Armored shorts, a companion piece to the vest, were issued to some units but were extraordinarily uncomfortable and seldom even seen, much less worn.

EVERYDAY LIFE

For the typical Marine in the I Corps region, everyday life was not typical garrison duty, but a succession of often boring routine duties performed under the constant nagging expectation of a random enemy attack. It was the realization of the old axiom that war is 90 percent boredom and 10 percent sheer terror.

Carlos arrived in the Republic of Vietnam with a planeload of strangers. Early units arrived in Vietnam as cohesive units, but the troop rotation policy meant a constant flow of inexperienced men like Carlos into the embattled country.

At the end of World War II the US military established a system under which men were awarded "points" based on length of time overseas, wounds, awards and decorations, family considerations (such as children), and other factors. The number of points determined the priority for repatriation. In Korea and in Vietnam men served a predetermined length of time in the combat zone. The term of service for

The first unit to arrive in South Vietnam was a platoon of tanks attached to the 9th Marine Expeditionary Brigade. The unit is shown loading ammunition while sighting in and test-firing the cannons of their tanks near Danang. (NARA)

a Marine in Vietnam was thirteen months, compared to twelve months for other branches of the service. The rotation system assured that no small group would bear the full burden of the war, but from a military point of view the system was detrimental to combat effectiveness and unit cohesion.

World War II and Korea demonstrated that survival in combat is in part a function of experience. Inexperienced replacements were more likely to become casualties. The greater the experience, the greater the chance of ultimate survival, and of course combat-experienced men were more effective, particularly at the NCO level.

The rotation policy guaranteed that novices continuously replaced experienced men. Men in the last quarter or so of their tour were said to be "short-timers" or just "short". Morale suffered because it was considered very bad luck for the unit as a whole if a man was killed or wounded when he was "short".

Carlos departed California with the summer dress uniform he was wearing, and with his utilities, skivvies, and a few personal items in his seabag. Like other Marines, Carlos flew by civilian airline from California, staging through Camp Hague on Okinawa, and on to Vietnam.

When Carlos landed at Danang his tropical dress uniform was carefully packed and placed in storage. Part-way through his tour he would be granted one to two weeks of Rest and Recreation leave, or R&R. At that time he could recover his dress uniform, required wear for R&R in such places as Manila, Hong Kong, or the greatest prize of all, Hawaii. The balance of a Marine's leave – thirty days per year – was taken before going to Vietnam, or accumulated for use after his tour.

Individual Marines were generally held at Danang until some unit requested a replacement for a casualty or a man returning to "the World". During this interval they might be assigned odd duties around the sprawling base. Warrant Officer Jim Carroll says that most new tankers guarded the big ammunition dump there until the tank units "whined and sniveled" for the men to be released to the tank companies.

A Military Policeman (wearing the camouflage uniform introduced in mid-1968) directs new arrivals at the III Marine Amphibious Corps Transit Center, Danang. The man on the left will soon be made to regret the general untidiness of his appearance. (USMCRC)

Life in a tank company

In due course, Carlos was assigned to Alpha Company, 1st Tank Battalion. The Company First Sergeant assigned him to a platoon, where he became a "snuffy", the tanker's unique term for a new man. Further orientation to life in Vietnam included a talk by the Company Gunny (both a rank, and the billet of the senior technical NCO in the company – see Glossary) on the little things that might help keep him alive. This included a lecture on enemy weapons, including a clever imitation of the odd "thunk" that indicates you have but seconds before a mortar shell arrives. The NVA and VC were very good with mortars, the gunny assured him.

Carlos was assigned to a veteran tank crew, headed by Sergeant Nicholas Berwick, a tall, lean, black Marine from North Carolina. Berwick was a "lifer", a long-service professional. Amiable but a strict disciplinarian, he had voluntarily extended his tour and was now in his fifteenth consecutive month in Vietnam.

Like all snuffies, Carlos was again subjected to generally good-natured torments and practical jokes. He also became, of course, the most junior member of the tank crew – the loader.

Each member of a tank crew is part of a miniature society, with clearly defined roles. Each plays a particular part in a complex physical ballet performed inside a closed steel box amid the roar of the engine and guns, pitching and rolling as it moves across rough terrain.

The senior man was the tank commander, or TC. In battle his task was to maintain a constant awareness of his surroundings and threats to his tank, acquire targets and point them out to the gunner, and specify how to attack them with a standardized fire command. A typical fire command would be "Gunner! HE [High Explosive]! Troops in open! Three hundred meters!" or "Gunner! Machine gun! Troops!" The gunner would call back "Identified!" When the loader replied "Up!" it indicated that he had loaded the correct projectile type, switched the loading safety to the off position, and the weapon was ready to fire.

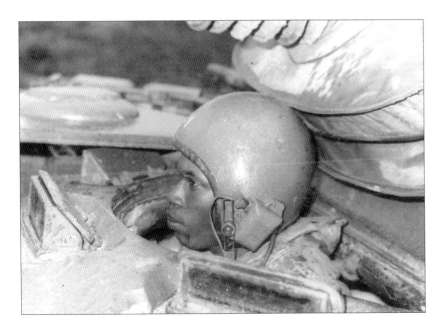

This photo of a typical tank driver illustrates the mud-encrusted driver's vision periscopes that often forced the driver to operate the tank either with his head exposed, or blind under the verbal directions of the tank commander. (NARA)

Master Gunnery Sergeant Don Gagnon: "When the tank commander says 'Fire!', and the gunner says 'On the way!', then Bang! Off goes the round." The tank commander also used his cupola machine gun to help defend the tank.

Most people have the perception that in combat the tank's crew is behind thick armor and secure from enemy small-arms fire. In fact, constant vigilance is the tank crew's most important defense. Warrant Officer Jim Carroll, a veteran of tank fighting on Iwo Jima in World War II, was a Platoon Leader in Vietnam. "In Vietnam the tank commander almost always rode unbuttoned, which of course gave you the greater advantage of visibility, to see what was going on and be able to direct your gunner where to shoot. The disadvantage is that if you've got a sniper in the area, he can pot you right there in the turret." 1st Tank Battalion units also remounted the TC's .50-cal. machine gun atop the cupola. Colonel 'Case' Casey, who spent 15 months in Vietnam as the Captain in charge of Alpha Company, explained that the cupola machine gun "was mounted on its side, and it fed in a ninety degree angle, and it would do nothing but jam. We just pulled that thing out of there … and sky-mounted the thing, where the TC had to pop up to fire it. And that was dangerous."

The gunner required a good working relationship with the TC. The TC had an override, a control that allowed him to seize control of the turret and gun and point it in the direction of a target the gunner might not have seen. To avoid working at cross purposes the gunner and TC had to coordinate their actions under extreme stress. The gunner and TC also had to work together to adjust fire. The gunner fired and the tank commander observed the fall of shot from his higher and more advantageous position, then gave the gunner verbal adjustments if he was blinded by dust or smoke. A good gunner also had to master the art of leading a moving target.

The loader had the most physically demanding job. He listened to the type of round specified in the TC's fire command, selected it from the ready ammunition racks, and wrestled the heavy and awkward rounds inside the cramped confines of the turret. The rounds, depending upon type, weighed from 31.44 to 44.67lb (14.3 to 20.3kg) and were 37.48 to 35.92in. (95.2 to 91.2cm) in length. The loader inserted the nose of the round into the main gun mechanism and jammed it forward using the heel of his closed fist, then snatched his hand out of the way before the breech closed automatically. He shouted "Up", and flattened his body against the side of the turret, out of the main gun's recoil path. As the gun fired and recoiled, mechanical extractors plucked the hot brass from the chamber. The loader stood ready to slap the emerging hot brass casing down onto the turret deck to avoid it bouncing around inside the turret, and was ready with the next round. Don Gagnon said, "It takes a lot of strength, understanding of what the tank commander wants, and once the tank commander gets a little excited and starts cussing at him he's got to let that flow off of him and continue to load the gun."

The loader was also responsible for reloading the .30.cal. coaxial machine gun, emptying the expended brass bag, and clearing any jams. To save time in combat the loader usually dumped the brass into an empty .50-cal. machine gun ammunition box and stowed it somewhere inside the turret. In his spare time the loader replenished the ready ammunition from the main ammunition storage racks.

The driver worked in physical isolation in the front of the tank. Although his primary responsibility was to steer the vehicle across the battlefield, he was poorly positioned for his task. His view was often blocked by tall vegetation. If he drove with the hatch open and his head exposed, he was inundated by rain, dust, or mud thrown up by his own or nearby vehicles. If he drove with his hatch closed, his view was restricted to that provided by several small periscopes which as likely as not were coated with dust, mud, rainwater, or damaged by small-arms fire. Often he drove by remote control, directed by the TC from his position atop the turret. An additional responsibility was to utilize his gauges to monitor the performance of the tank's engine and electrical systems.

One of the most enervating factors that differentiated the war in Vietnam from America's other wars of the twentieth century was that, as in all guerrilla wars, combat could not be readily separated from everyday life. Guard posts and essential convoys were routinely attacked, even along the most heavily patrolled highways. "Secure" base camps were subject to attack by long-range rockets and infiltration by suicidal sapper teams. Safety was achieved only when Marines left the country, either through repatriation at the end of their tour of duty, or during the brief R&R period.

Otherwise life in a base area could be little different from that in some training areas back in the States. Long-term housing was in large tents or in plywood huts with canvas or corrugated metal roofs. The low walls came only to about waist height, with the upper part screened to allow a cooling breeze while keeping out the clouds of mosquitoes and flies. Sandbag walls separated the buildings and provided protective revetments in case of mortar or rocket attack. Folding cots provided a predictable, if not always comfortable, sleeping arrangement.

Administrative offices, laundries, mess halls, a Post Exchange, and even clubs – segregated by rank into Enlisted Men's, NCO, Staff NCO, and Officers' clubs – rounded out the amenities of any large base.

Marines quickly acquired or manufactured luxuries that might make life more bearable. These ranged from radios or tape decks for playing music (available at low cost through the PX system), to the occasional electric washing machine purchased on the local civilian market. Charcoal-fueled cooking grills, made by splitting an old fuel barrel,

Although tours by famous entertainers like the late Bob Hope garnered most of the publicity, lesser-known entertainers provided the vast majority of shows. This troupe is "Miss Jacqie Darnell and Nashville Vietnam". (USMCRC)

allowed the troops to cook hot dogs, hamburgers, and the occasional steak to relieve the tedium of mess hall food.

Even in a war zone junior men like Carlos were subject to the constant grind of small, sometimes humiliating, tasks necessary to the operation of any large military base. Units were required to supply men for such mundane tasks as mess duty, collecting and burning trash, and the general cleanup referred to as police duty.

Worst of all was head (latrine) duty, often assigned as punishment. The heads were screened plywood buildings, fitted with simple seats consisting of holes cut through a sheet of plywood. Urine and excrement were collected in low metal tubs made of a 55-gallon fuel drum cut in half, with two handholds cut out of the sides of the half-barrel. A small amount of diesel fuel was poured into each drum, and floated on top of the waste. This measure reduced the odor only minimally, and had little effect on the flies. The unlucky few assigned to this unpalatable duty circulated with a jeep and trailer, hauling the filled cylinders away to be emptied and cleaned by simply lighting the fuel. Worse than the actual work was the occasional taunt of "Hey, buddy. Whad'ya do to get assigned to that shit detail?"

Everyday life was a mind-numbing succession of routine offensive and defensive operations, interrupted by periods of intense and often terrifying combat. In contrast to the Army doctrine of using tanks en masse, Marine tanks were generally assigned in small groups under the operational control of an infantry unit. When employed defensively tanks provided heavy firepower for the protection of key locations such as bridges, or acted as reaction forces that were assigned to rush to the aid of isolated positions under attack. Proactive defensive operations included providing security for the combat engineers who each morning swept key roads for mines planted each night by guerrillas, and providing escorts for road convoys.

No matter what the assignment, the men's daily lives revolved around the maintenance requirements of the tank. The tanks required constant care under the best of conditions, and Vietnam provided extremes of climatic and physical conditions unfriendly to tanks. In the wet season the tanks bogged down in deep mud, and water seeped in through every opening to corrode metal or damage electrical components. In the dry season clouds of fine dust and sand clogged engine air filters and found their way into bearings and other moving parts. Simply keeping the tanks in operation was a daily struggle, in addition to the one against the enemy. Routine maintenance took on increased importance.

One of the tank commander's jobs was to maintain the vehicle logbook, a continuous record of how many hours the tank was operated each day (a special clock was provided), rounds fired, cleaning, and routine maintenance performed. One such routine task was cleaning the air filters, sometimes several times each day. Abrasive dust constantly clogged the filters housed in boxes on the fenders. Cleaning them required opening the box and removing the heavy multi-baffle filters, then plugging the main air ducts that led from the filter box into the engine. The filters were cleaned by beating them against the side of the tank, knocking loose the dust and fine sand, and in the process raising another cloud of choking dust.

The men also suffered from the dust, particularly during the dry season. Any movement by the tanks churned up choking clouds of fine

powder, and driving for miles in the plume of dust could cause respiratory or eye problems.

Like the infantry, tank crews spent a great deal of time in isolated positions. This meant that meals consisted largely of a monotonous succession of canned C-rations. "C"s came in 22lb (10kg) cardboard crates of twelve meals, a mix of several menus. A typical meal, individually boxed, centered about a canned entrée – spaghetti and meatballs, ham and lima beans, scrambled eggs with ham, spiced beef, pork steak, beans and franks, chicken and noodles, turkey loaf, or sliced beef. Although individuals had their own preferences, certain of the entrées were widely detested – ham and lima beans for its tendency to induce flatulence, and ham and eggs for the soggy texture. Each package included canned bread crisps ("John Wayne crackers"), and a packet of condiments. A sweet was provided in the form of canned fruit (typically peaches, apricots, or mixed fruit) or canned pound cake (a heavy, buttery confection). Canned apricots were banned in the 3d Tank Battalion because superstition held that they caused mechanical breakdowns. Other items included small cans of cheese spread, jellies, and grainy peanut butter.

The boxed meal also included chewing gum, a plastic spoon, a small packet of toilet paper, matches, and a packet of four cigarettes. A few folding metal can openers, called P-38s, came packed in each crate. The typical Marine acquired one of these useful items and carried it on the neck chain with his dog tags.

In theory three C-rations provided a nutritionally balanced and adequate daily diet of 3,300 calories, but the selection grew extraordinarily monotonous. To dress up the Cs, Marines often acquired or made up individual condiment kits. One popular supplement was a bottle of McIlhenny's Tabasco Sauce®, a spicy red pepper sauce manufactured on Avery Island, Louisiana. (As a junior officer, Brigadier General Walter S. McIlhenny USMCR won the Navy Cross on Guadalcanal in Word War II).

Hot A- and B-rations were transported to the field in large insulated cans, and typically eaten from the individual's mess tin. The man at left has obtained a steel mess tray for his personal use. (USMCRC)

The tedium of C-rations was relieved by A- or B-rations, cooked rations comparable to a cafeteria meal. Prepared by unit cooks and bakers, they were served in a base area mess hall or carried to the field in large insulated cans. In the field A- and B-rations were normally eaten from the folding mess kit issued as part of the 782 gear, but it was not uncommon for tankers to make off with one of the mess hall's heavy stamped-steel dining trays for personal use in the field.

The sole concession to civilized life was a one-can-per-day beer ration. Like other Marines, the tankers sometimes managed to hoard several cans to drink at one time.

Bridge guard

"Case" Casey complained that for tanks "The primary responsibility was guarding bridges. They were using those doggone vehicles as a mobile pillbox. They would run that thing out there, and set it on a bridge."

Bridge guard was not a very popular duty among the enlisted men either. One or two tanks, along with an infantry detachment, would be tasked to guard a particularly important bridge. During daylight the tanks would sight their guns on likely routes of enemy approach and record relative azimuths and elevations. The relative azimuth (the angular relationship between the direction the main gun was pointing and the fore-and-aft axis of the tank's hull) was determined from an indicator in the turret. In darkness the gunner could simply align the guns on these predetermined targets and open fire. The tanks could also use their searchlights to illuminate the area, since their position was usually no secret to potential attackers.

The relatively quiet duty might turn into weeks of tedium, sitting idly in the baking heat or rain, and subject to the constant nagging expectation of an attack. To relieve the boredom the crew could occasionally crank up the tank and drive to the company position to replenish fuel and ammunition, get a shower and a hot meal, and then return to their lonely outpost.

At other times the company gunny or the platoon sergeant sent out supplies of food and ammunition, clothing, and other items. Don Gagnon recalled his best platoon sergeant, O.K. Martin, a big Texan usually identified by a bulging wad of chewing tobacco. Martin would wander in, typically with his utilities in rags from sliding around on the rough casting surfaces of the tank, to the usual demand of the company gunny to get cleaned up. Martin would refuse, saying, "Not until my troops have been taken care of." Then he would commandeer a truck or a jeep with a trailer, load it down with supplies, and be back on the road to provide for his men.

On these lengthy assignments the tank crews would make themselves as comfortable as possible with cots, folding chairs, tape decks, and other homey luxuries. The more resourceful might even acquire a few sheets of plywood and build a small building or "hooch" against one side of the tank to sleep more comfortably.

In some cases sections of tanks were also assigned to forward base camps or artillery firebases to help protect them from attacks. Tying down the tanks on stationary duties like bridge guard and base security was not popular with the leadership of the tank battalions, who decried the practice with a little ditty about "Two on the bridge and three on the ridge."

Convoy escort and road security

Truck convoys were subject to ambush even on main routes, so tanks were sometimes assigned to escort them. The VC proved more than willing to ambush American tanks. Army General Donn Starry, the primary authority on Army tanks in Vietnam, wrote that "it could be boring, tedious, and in the minds of many a waste of armored vehicles. When it was done poorly, or the enemy was determined to oppose it, it was dangerous, disorganized, and again in the minds of many, a one-way ride to disaster." Jim Carroll put it more succinctly. "We were channelized on the roads, which was a dangerous thing, because if they know where you're coming from, if they've got anybody that's got any balls, they're gonna have them out there with these RPGs [Rocket Propelled Grenades, actually a primitive anti-tank missile launcher]."

The VC continually mined the roads, and mines were a far greater threat than ambushes. Starry noted that in one typical six-month period, 73 percent of all tank losses were to mines. Each morning small teams of combat engineers, sometimes escorted by tanks, searched the roads for newly laid mines. Some were locally made mines with a crude pressure plate trigger. Others were powerful devices rigged from unexploded aircraft bombs and electrically detonated by a VC hiding in the nearby countryside.

Case Casey spoke of convoy duty. "Every time they would do that, we'd end up losing at least one tank, out of a section or platoon, to mines. What the infantry wanted to do was put that tank out front, put all the trucks behind it, and let that tank clear the mines. It would clear them all right. A very expensive mine detector, but that's exactly what they wanted to do."

Command-detonated mines were the primary threat to tanks. On August 16, 1967, tanker Richard D. Carey was manning a machine gun on a truck from the H&S Company of 3d Tank Battalion, helping a platoon of tanks escort a supply convoy from the big base at Phu Bai, through Hue City to Camp Evans, and back again along the well-traveled Highway One. As they waited inside the main gate of Camp Evans for the return trip, Carey chatted with his friends in the crew of one tank. He walked away as the tank drove out the gate of the base. Moments later there was a titanic explosion: the tank had struck a command-detonated mine on the very outskirts of the base, at a spot they had traversed just hours before.

Tanks from Alpha Company, 3d Tank Battalion bypass a bridge near Con Thien. Richard Carey witnessed the complete destruction of a tank by a command-detonated mine on a similar bypass immediately outside Camp Evans. (USMCRC)

When Carey and others rushed over, he saw the tank upside down with the wheels and tracks blown off, the hull torn open. The turret lay 50ft (15m) away. The four friends he had just been talking with had died instantly. "As I turned to get away from the scene, I caught out of the corner of my eye a body on the ground. I don't remember seeing any blood but I do remember the body was completely void of any clothing or equipment." Carey made the long trip back to Phu Bai in a state of shock.

No place, or time, in Vietnam was completely safe.

Reaction platoon

Carlos's own introduction to random danger came with his assignment to a reaction platoon. These were usually ad hoc formations, and might include tanks from different platoons. Most nights the assignment was routine. Then one night the VC attacked an infantry company on a nearby hill.

When Carlos's tank commander, Sergeant Berwick, went to wake the designated reaction platoon leader, he had been drinking so the disgusted Berwick took charge of the reaction platoon himself.

On previous trips to familiarize themselves with the ground, the tanks had taken the same route out to the hill. A broad churned-up path marked their usual route. Berwick felt that something was amiss, and headed off cross-country with the other tanks trailing behind. Without night vision devices, the tank commanders and drivers rode with their heads exposed. As the tanks passed down slope from a sharp bend in the usual tank trail, RPG anti-tank rockets came arcing wildly out of the darkness and exploded harmlessly in the underbrush. Enemy rocket gunners had been waiting in ambush, precisely where the tanks would have slowed to negotiate a turn in the usual trail.

Approaching the infantry position the tank crews could clearly see the defensive perimeter in the flickering white light of mortar illumination rounds, and ringed about with green and red tracers.

Berwick keyed his radio, quickly advised his tank commanders of his plan, and the small tank column barged through the encircling ring of

enemy, into the embattled perimeter. Berwick and the other tank commanders stood high up in their cupolas, hosing the underbrush with their machine guns.

In the middle of the perimeter was a large sandbagged tent used for a command post and radio position. In the flickering light the sergeant glimpsed dark figures moving around the tent.

"Gunner! Tent. Enemy infantry, HE!"

Knowles, the gunner, hesitated, unsure he had heard his tank commander correctly. To make sure, he replied "Tent! Identified!"

Unable to see what was happening, Carlos had no such qualms. He slammed the round into the chamber and shouted "Up!"

The gunner shouted "On the wa-a-a-ay!" and depressed the electrical trigger on his control handle. The protracted shout allowed Berwick to close his eyes, and protect what remained of his night vision from the muzzle flash. The tank bucked as the main gun fired. When the breech of the main gun flew backward and ejected the hot brass casing, Carlos slapped it down onto the deck, just as he had been taught.

Fragments of the tent and its contents – human and otherwise – rained down on the perimeter. Satisfied that the target was neutralized, Berwick searched for others. Ducking down into the interior of his cupola, he twisted the commander's override handle, slewing the turret around until he could see the origin of a stream of green tracers through his periscope.

"Gunner! Enemy machine gun! Machine gun!"

"Identified!" Knowles sent a stream of rounds out into the darkness, using the tracers to walk it onto the target. Carlos heard only the yammering of the machine gun near his ear, and the clatter of brass into the collecting bag.

For Carlos the next hour was an exhausting blur of slamming rounds into the main gun, heaving the hot brass shell casings out his overhead hatch, linking new belts of ammunition to the coaxial machine gun, and repeatedly emptying the heavy canvas bag that collected the machine-gun brass. Carlos accomplished most of these tasks by instinct alone. He was blinded by tears and light-headed from the propellant fumes that leaked out of the machine-gun and cannon breeches, and the heat and metallic stench of the expended brass.

At first light Berwick called for Carlos to dismount with him, and they walked over to the wreckage of the squad tent. In the smoldering rubble were charred and dismembered bodies, as well as AK-47 assault rifles and other enemy weapons.

"Standard VC tactic," explained Berwick. "Infiltrate a squad before the shooting starts, and when things get hot and heavy, attack the weakest part of the perimeter from the inside. Blow a hole, and all your buddies flood in. They were using the tent as a rally point." Berwick kicked one of the weapons, and walked away.

Another "routine" night had ended.

FIELD OPERATIONS

In Vietnam there were no distinct campaigns separated by periods of R&R, only periods of uneasy watchfulness punctuated by search operations designed to locate and destroy the elusive enemy. This war was very much akin to the ones the Marines had fought against the Creek Indians in Alabama and Georgia (1836), the Seminole Indians in Florida (1836–38), and Filipino insurrectionists (1899–1902). Offensive operations in Vietnam were intended to destroy the enemy's base areas and to disrupt his plans for offensive action. These often brought the Marines into contact with the VC Main Force Battalions.

VC Main Force Battalions, recruited from local village cadres and equipped with heavy weapons, were not part-time warriors, but permanently organized units. The senior leadership, and many of the rank and file, had been engaged in warfare since 1945. The Marines faced a foe that combined the invisibility of the guerrilla with the professionalism and striking power of a veteran conventional army.

Both the American and Communist leadership made complementary – and fateful – decisions in 1967 that would have catastrophic consequences. General William C. Westmoreland planned to bring the enemy to a climactic battle, where he could destroy them with firepower. To that end American forces would pursue the enemy into his remote base areas. General Vo Nguyen Giap wanted to lure the Americans into the remote areas along the Laotian border, where American mechanized firepower and mobility would be largely nullified by the rugged terrain. There the NVA could "bleed them without mercy." The VC would continue to operate against the American and RVN forces in the populated areas.

In response to Communist pressure, III Amphibious Corps began to realign many of its units. When such organizational shuffles occurred, men like Carlos seldom knew what unit they were operating with, or the names of the operations in which they were involved. They knew only that their platoon or section of tanks was assigned to cooperate with some infantry company or battalion for a brief and often confusing period.

(continued on page 41)

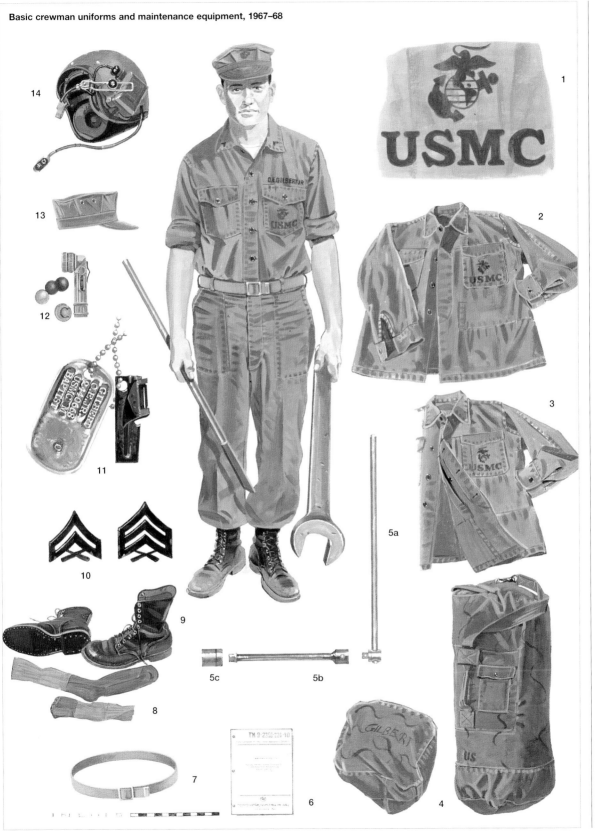

B

Pugil stick drill, late stage of recruit training

Vehicle maintenance and repair equipment

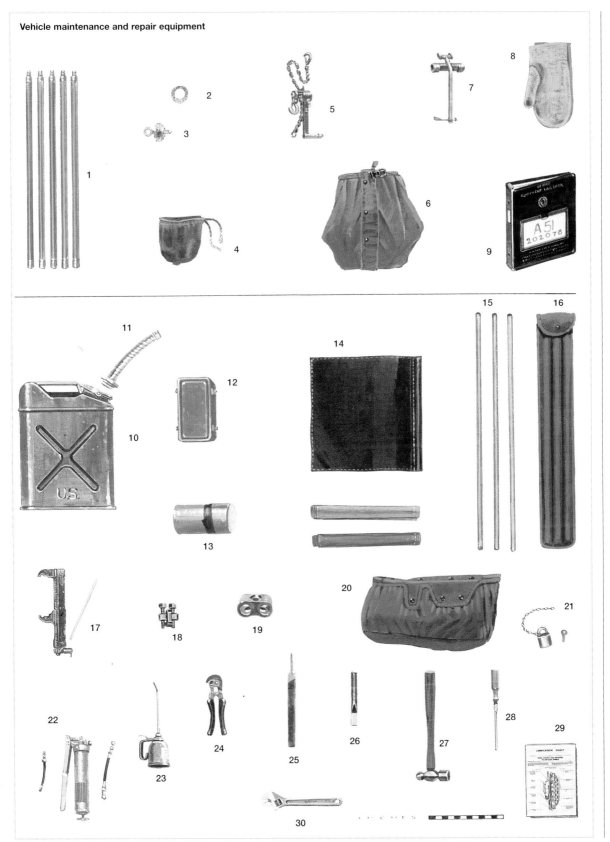

c

Combat tactics and action, south of Marble Mountain

D

Urban combat, Tet Offensive, 1968

F

After battle – immediate medical attention and first aid

Basic crewman uniform and equipment, Republic of Vietnam

Search and destroy

In late 1967 the VC launched a terrorist attack against a refugee camp south of Danang, killing over a hundred civilians. On November 13 the 1st Marine Division launched Operation Foster, a sweep by two infantry battalions to locate and punish the VC unit responsible. Smaller operations sought to flush out and destroy enemy units in nearby areas, and one of these provided Carlos's first experience of sustained combat.

South of Danang and the nearby air facility at Marble Mountain was a roadless and inaccessible strip of coastline with low wooded hills, salt marshes and tidal streams, sandy lowlands and small, scattered villages. For decades such natural base areas, difficult to enter unannounced, but nestled close to major population centers, were hotbeds of guerrilla activity.

The area was to be searched by tanks and infantry, supported by a unit of big box-like amphibian tractors, called amtracs, which on land served the Marines as armored personnel carriers. This force combed the uneven hills and scrub woodlands for days. Occasionally a tank was called upon to loose a few rounds of 90mm or a burst of machine-gun fire into some wood line where the enemy offered resistance.

On one typical day a prisoner, under none too gentle interrogation, revealed the position of a bunker dug into a nearby hillside. The initial approach was met with heavy fire, so Berwick's two-tank section was called up. Sitting atop the turret in the noonday heat, Carlos had a ringside seat as the other tank went into action.

The tank commander stood upright in his cupola, with an infantry sergeant riding on the deck behind

ABOVE **1st Tank Battalion tankers observe artillery fire directed against a tree line on a sweep operation south of Danang. Note the tank commander's armored vest kept close at hand, and the sandbagged machine-gun tripod atop the cupola. (NARA)**

LEFT **The big box-like LVTP-5 amphibian tractor served as a personnel carrier on land. The fuel tanks in the floor made it highly vulnerable to mines, so the infantry preferred to ride on top. The vehicle at left is an Ontos tank destroyer. (USMCRC)**

41

the turret to provide direction and point out the target. The rest of the infantry platoon settled down to watch, happy to let the tank do the work.

The big main gun slammed out a round, the muzzle blast raising a cloud of white dust from the sandy soil. The tank loosed another round at the target, and then a third. Carlos could hear the deafening crack of the cannon, and the almost immediate explosion somewhere behind the small hill in front of him. A cloud of white smoke billowed out of the loader's hatch of the other tank. The loader in the other tank had left his hatch open because the fume extractor, designed to minimize the backflow of hot gasses generated by the main gun's propellant charges, often allowed smoke to flow back into the turret.

The infantry sergeant hit the tank commander between the shoulder blades twice with his fist, and turned to motion the infantry forward. The grunts wearily saddled up and moved in, prodding the hapless prisoner in front of them. The show was over.

That night brought little rest. Operations continued until twilight, when the tankers grabbed a quick bite to eat and began maintenance procedures that continued well into the night. The crews grabbed what sleep they could since two men from each tank had to be on watch to guard against a night attack. The occasional incoming mortar round or burst of automatic weapon fire reduced rest to a matter of two hours each night – if they were lucky.

After a week, Carlos was functioning in an exhausted daze. The baking heat further debilitated the crews. Rumor had it that the temperatures were over 105 °F (41 °C), and it was far hotter inside the tanks. Small tasks like clearing jams in the coaxial machine gun required intense concentration.

Even the more experienced crewmen and the fastidious Sergeant Berwick made serious mistakes. The crew rose before dawn and staggered about readying the tank. Berwick was checking in with the distant company headquarters by radio when the driver climbed in and cranked the engine. Berwick snatched his helmet off and let loose with a blistering stream of obscenities. He should have turned off the radio, because the power surge might have destroyed the radio.

Sweep operations required clearing one tree line after another, each a potential ambush site. Tank C-33 from Charlie Company, 1st Tank Battalion supports infantry from 3d Battalion, 1st Marines in action south of Marble Mountain. (USMCRC)

That day a Main Force unit reinforced the local VC cadre, and Mister Charles – the nickname the Marines used for the enemy when he was particularly skillful or tenacious – turned to fight. The war was evolving into one of attrition, where success was measured by the body count of enemy dead. Both sides "piled on," and threw in reinforcements in the hope of inflicting crippling casualties, killing for the sake of killing.

The Marine infantry doggedly attacked throughout the hot day, and were repeatedly repulsed. Casualties mounted. By midday Carlos's tank had expended its full load of ammunition, and was ordered to fall back to a landing zone where helicopters were bringing in a resupply.

A 3d Tank Battalion tank helps secure a landing zone during a sweep operation. The helicopters brought in essentials like food, water, ammunition, and sometimes fuel for the tanks, and carried away the wounded. (USMCRC)

A blood-spattered medical corpsman commandeered the tank to transport the dead to the LZ. For minutes that seemed like endless hours, Carlos helped drag the unwieldy green plastic body bags onto the engine deck. Some of the bags were already beginning to swell in the relentless heat.

At the LZ the bags were unloaded and stacked, and the crew began the backbreaking task of replenishing main-gun ammunition. Each of the 62 heavy cannon rounds had to be broken out of its wooden packing crate, removed from a waterproof fiberboard tube closed by heavy tape, and stowed inside the tank. For the return trip the tanks were loaded down with white plastic water containers, which were quickly stained by mud and blood from the deck of the tank.

All the while amphibian tractors shuttled back and forth carrying more wounded Marines, who waited patiently in the stifling heat. Just as one of the helicopters lifted off with a load of critically wounded men, Carlos heard a characteristic thunking sound, like someone hitting a piece of drainpipe. Seconds later explosions bracketed the helicopter, and Carlos watched in horror as it spewed smoke and slammed into the ground. Marines on the ground ran in to drag the wounded back out of the doors.

The next day brought more battering against the hills, and more casualties. Carlos's tank was leading a column of amtracs, seeking to outflank a hill. The tanks often led the columns because they were far less vulnerable to anti-tank weapons and mines than the thinly armored tractors.

Just as the tank nosed out into a broad clearing, the front of the tank suddenly lurched upward with a resounding "whump", and a cloud of choking dust filled the interior. The tank continued forward under its own momentum for a short distance, and lurched to a stop. It had struck a mine buried in the sandy soil.

The mine inflicted little damage, breaking the track on the right side, and slightly damaging the forward road wheels, but not breaking the torsion bar or the road wheel support arm. Regardless of the minimal damage, the net result was that the tank was out of action.

Sweep or "search and destroy" operations were the "campaigns" of the Vietnam War. The infantry on the rear deck helped protect the tank's blind spots against potential attackers hidden in the tall grass. (USMCRC)

A bent suspension arm would have required them to "short track" the tank. This procedure required removing damaged road wheels and damaged sections of track, then shortening the remaining track so that the tank could run on only five road wheels per side, rather than the usual six.

While another tank protected them, the crew worked to replace the damaged track sections with the spares carried on the turret sides. Wrestling the heavy track in the sandy soil and baking heat was grueling labor.

In the late afternoon the entire tank platoon was ordered to escort a group of amtracs loaded with body bags and "walking wounded" back along a winding trail to a logistics point outside the battle area. Berwick switched the duties around, and Carlos took over the TC's position, his first time to do so "in country".

As the column passed a tree line that had been secured days earlier, the vehicles were suddenly swept by heavy machine-gun fire. RPG rockets arced out of the trees, disabling the lead tank. Wounded Marines tumbled off the tractors and began to return fire as mortar rounds rained down upon them, killing and wounding the already injured. Over his radio Carlos heard both the tank platoon leader and the officer in charge of the wounded calling desperately for help. From the gunner's position Berwick began to fire into the tree line. Carlos himself stood high up in the cupola and hammered away with the roof-mounted .50-cal. machine gun.

While the attention of the tank crews was riveted on the tree line, enemy sappers, hidden in the tall grass, rose up and rushed in to attack the tanks from their blind spot, the side away from the trees. The first indication Carlos had that his tank was under attack came when, from the corner of his eye, he saw two figures armed with AK-47s and satchel charges climb up onto the engine deck. Unable to swing the big machine gun around, Carlos screamed at Knowles to close the loader's hatch, while he groped for his .45-cal. pistol.

The two enemy sappers dove behind the back of the turret, just as Carlos loosed two rounds from his pistol at them. They crouched there while Carlos cowered behind the hatch section of the armored cupola that folded back to form a seat. It was a stand-off – neither could attack the other.

"Get Alexander in the tank behind us," Berwick instructed from inside the turret. "Tell him to scratch our back."

"What?"

"Just do it!" shouted Berwick.

Carlos relayed the unfamiliar instruction, and watched as the turret of the tank behind turned to point directly at him.

With a loud curse Berwick grabbed Carlos by the belt and jerked him down into the turret, just as Alexander's .30-cal. machine-gun fire began to hammer on the rear of the turret and cupola, sweeping away the two

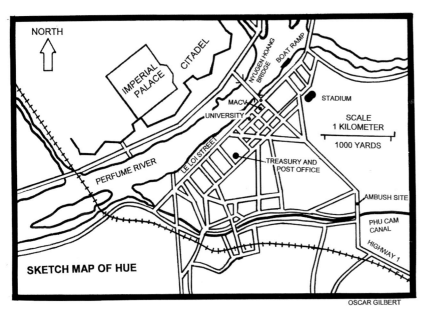

sappers. Scratching each other's backs was a desperate measure used by Marine Corps tankers to counter Japanese suicide attackers during World War II.

The rest of the afternoon was anti-climactic for the tank crews, as the enemy attackers broke contact soon after. For the infantry, the worst fighting was yet to come. The ambush of the column had been a bloody diversion, executed to trigger a much larger ambush of the Marine infantry company that rushed to their rescue.

COMBAT – THE TET OFFENSIVE

In the early years of the war Tet, the Vietnamese Lunar New Year holiday, was generally observed as a truce by both sides. On the first night of Tet 1968, 30/31 January, the Communists struck at every major city in South Vietnam, and attacked most of the larger American bases.

Hue, the old Imperial capital and the cultural center of the nation, was a city of 140,000 inhabitants spread along both banks of the Perfume River. On the north side of the river the massive brick walls of the Citadel fortress encircled the old city. The newer French colonial part of the city on the south bank had broad boulevards, parks, palatial homes with walled gardens, and sturdy masonry buildings.

Hue also held strategic importance. Highway One – the main north–south supply route from the big logistics base at Danang and the combat base at Phu Bai, to bases in the north – and the country's main north–south railway both crossed the river in Hue. The Navy Boat Ramp on the navigable Perfume River was a major unloading facility for heavy cargo.

The first days
The city was essentially undefended and untouched by the war. Within a few hours nine battalions of VC and NVA troops seized control of the city. Only two major enclaves held out – the Military Assistance

Command Vietnam (MACV) compound located in a converted hotel building on the south bank, and the ARVN 1st Division Headquarters on the north bank.

The two Marine divisions were caught off balance. The 3d Marine Division was in the process of displacing to the extreme north of the country, and as a result the 1st Marine Division was modifying its Tactical Area of Responsibility (TAOR). The 1st Marine Division had established Task Force X-Ray, a temporary forward headquarters under Brigadier General Foster C. LaHue, at the Phu Bai Combat Base south of Hue.

The first American unit to stumble into the battle for Hue was a provisional platoon of four tanks from the 3d Tank Battalion that was headed for the Navy Boat Ramp.

On Highway One just outside Hue the platoon encountered a group of ARVN M-41 tanks and M113 personnel carriers that had been ambushed. The body of one Vietnamese TC was still upright in his hatch, burned to a grisly black caricature.

The tanks also encountered a convoy of trucks carrying the infantry of Alpha Company, 1st Battalion, 1st Marines. The infantry officer, Captain Gordon Batcheller, was under orders from Task Force X-Ray to move through the city on a reconnaissance. Batcheller commandeered the tanks and loaded his infantry aboard.

The small command was soon pinned down at the edge of the city. Automatic weapons fire and RPG rockets raked the tanks at point-blank range, damaging one tank and inflicting heavy losses on the infantry. At Phu Bai Lieutenant Colonel Marcus Gravel, the CO of 1st Battalion, 1st Marines, assembled a hasty relief force of his Headquarters Group and Golf Company 2/5, and set off to the rescue. Gravel would be the senior officer present in the city and control the growing Marine force.

By the time Gravel arrived, part of Alpha 1/1 and two of the tanks had fought their way clear of the ambush and set off cross-country to rescue the men trapped at the MACV Compound. By mid-afternoon Gravel's main force fought its way through to the MACV and secured the area.

With road communication with Phu Bai constantly interrupted by ambushes and mines, the Marines established a landing zone at the Boat Ramp for helicopters to bring in supplies and replacements and evacuate the wounded. Heavy machine-gun fire from across the river was directed at the helicopters until cannon fire from the tanks silenced the enemy guns, allowing air operations to proceed. The Marines held the area around the MACV Compound and the Boat Ramp, but the blocks of buildings in between were still infested with VC and NVA who attacked vehicles hauling wounded to the landing zone. Sometimes the cost of transporting a load of wounded to the LZ was another six or seven wounded or dead Marines. The tanks simply smashed a path through buildings so that the evacuation vehicles would not be so exposed to enemy fire in the open streets.

The provisional platoon experienced the loss of the only tank completely destroyed in the battle for

The walls of The Citadel are visible on the right (north) bank of the river, and Le Loi Street parallels the left bank. The Nyugen Hoang Bridge is nearest the viewer, and the MACV Compound and University are adjacent to the traffic circle in the foreground. (NARA)

Hue. During the fighting around the Boat Ramp one of the tanks took a hit from a powerful crew-served recoilless gun, the resulting explosion blowing the turret off the tank and killing the crew.

In the early morning hours of February 2 enemy sappers set off demolition charges wired to the Nyugen Hoang Bridge, and dropped one span into the river, thereby isolating the struggles for the north and south banks into two separate battles.

Alpha Company tanks in Hue

Captain "Case" Casey's Alpha Company, 1st Tank Battalion soon relieved the unlucky provisional platoon. Casey's 1st Platoon and infantry landed from LCUs (Landing Craft Utility) at a small boat ramp near the northeast corner of the Citadel, on the north bank. The NVA controlled both banks of the river, and Casey said, "The doggone U-boats were just devastated trying to come up the Perfume into Hue. There were two or three LCU hulks all up and down that thing. They weren't so bad when they noticed there were tanks on there, but when those U-boats were coming in loaded with ammunition, they could stand by. That was nothing but a death run up there."

Casey's 2d Platoon, reinforced with parts of his Headquarters Platoon, landed on the south bank at the Navy Boat Ramp. The LCUs could accommodate only three large vehicles, and the first boat carried two gun tanks and an M51 tank recovery vehicle. Although seldom mentioned in accounts of tank battles, the repair vehicles are essential and often accompany the first combat units into battle.

The sight that greeted Carlos and the other newly arrived tankers was hardly reassuring. The gutted and burned 3d Battalion tank sat near the Boat Ramp, with its charred turret lying several meters away. Casey recalled: "When the thing first started, Third Tank Battalion had a heavy section of tanks in there, and they lost one due to sympathetic detonation. It hit those rounds [stored] in that turret, and that booger just went up. That old tank hull was still sitting there on the ramp at Hue City when we got in there."

Casey had further cause to curse the continued use of his tanks as bridge guards. "That's the reason I never could get my other five tanks, my Third Platoon, up there. Division had them hung up on bridges down there, around Danang."

To simplify control and logistics, two five-vehicle platoons of Ontos tank destroyers belonging to the infantry units were placed under Casey's tactical control. Casey would have to fight one of the most protracted and savage battles of the war with only 11 gun tanks, 2 flame

Early in the battle for Hue enemy sappers destroyed the Nyugen Hoang Bridge, isolating Captain Case Casey's 3d Platoon tanks on the old city side from his main force on the south side. The south side is the far bank in this photo. (USMCRC)

The Chinese-made 57mm recoilless gun was a far more powerful anti-tank weapon than the RPG. A round from one of these guns was responsible for the loss of the only tank completely destroyed during the fighting in Hue. (USMCRC)

tanks, the VTR, and ten of the small Ontos, divided into two isolated forces by the demolition of the bridge.

Casey also lacked key support vehicles, particularly those needed to support his flame tanks. He had only a communications jeep, his personal jeep, and four trucks to support his scattered units on both banks of the river.

The thinly armored Ontos were, as Casey explained, "awfully vulnerable. If it's hit just right, a thirty caliber will go right through it. If it's hit with an RPG, it's just mayhem." The Ontos were used in a hit-and-run role; the small vehicle would race forward, loose its rounds, and then beat a rapid retreat.

Through the early days of February both sides continued to reinforce the units already inside the city, the Marines by helicopter airlift, and the NVA by infiltration through the western approaches until US Army forces closed off that route. The NVA sent in five more battalions of heavily armed and battle-hardened infantry.

The Marine force that would ultimately bear the full weight of the battle against 14 NVA and VC battalions consisted of the 1st Battalion, 1st Marines, the 1st and 2d Battalions, 5th Marines, and Casey's small armored force. All the units in Hue would be under the control of 1st Marines Headquarters, which was in turn under Task Force X-Ray.

The weather also conspired against the Marines. The low clouds and the low-hanging *crachin* fog limited air support in the first phases of the battle. In addition, the ARVN was at first reluctant to allow the use of artillery and tactical aircraft to attack enemy positions inside the historic city. The handful of tanks and Ontos were the only available heavy firepower.

The Marines on the south bank set about the task of systematically isolating and crushing the enemy forces inside that part of the city. Attacks east secured the Hue Stadium, and the open area was converted into a helicopter landing zone, where casualties were evacuated and supplies of food and ammunition accumulated in huge piles.

Attacks southwestward along the broad Le Loi Street that bordered the river, and westward along the banks of the Phu Cam Canal, isolated the wedge-shaped part of the city that sat between the two waterways. Patrols swept the areas between, and battled with infiltrators who crept back into the "cleared" areas of the city.

Dwindling bands of Marine riflemen, tank crewmen, and medical personnel were wounded and killed in the execution of each small step of this grand plan. The broad parks and boulevards provided excellent fields of fire for the defenders inside masonry buildings. When the Marines managed to break into each cluster of buildings, the battle was house-to-house, room-to-room.

Tanks were used to smash down the masonry walls that separated the back gardens of the large houses, so that the infantry could move forward through the enclosed gardens instead of along the fire-swept streets.

Tanks often led the attacks across open areas, but primarily used their 90mm cannons as assault artillery. Casey remarked: "That thing would knock a doggone hole – depending on what the building was made out of – you could almost knock a hole in there big enough to drive a jeep through. Particularly if you got a good hit on it. Sometimes it would go right through the masonry, and then explode inside the building." Both results saved the lives of the outnumbered infantrymen. "We used ninety per cent HE. We did have some flechette, and we used that when we could get a good shot on some of those troops. That was a deadly round too."

The flechette round was designed to replace the old canister round used to attack infantry in the open. Canister fired round steel balls that only had a short effective range, as the balls tended to fly in broad curves. The flechette round spewed out thousands of small, finned, steel darts, each about $1\frac{1}{2}$ in. (4cm) long. The darts flew straighter toward the target, had a longer range, and shredded flesh when they struck. The troops called it the "beehive" round because of the buzzing sound the darts made in flight.

Only rarely did the tank crewmen actually see the defenders, but on one occasion Berwick spotted a group of NVA moving across a broad, open park. It was the single occasion when he fired a flechette round. Berwick

ABOVE **An infantry squad follows a tank down a narrow side street on the south side of Hue. Snarls of fallen or dangling telephone and electrical wires, like those along the right side of this street, presented a potentially fatal hazard to unwary turret crewmen. (USMCRC)**

LEFT **Operations in built-up areas, like Hue and this area near Con Thien, presented the tankers with a three-dimensional battlefield. Danger might come from any side, or from above. The sniper's bullet was the greatest danger to tank commanders. (USMCRC)**

watched as the cloud of projectiles flew toward the target, and most of the running figures were bowled over in a spray of blood. The steel darts nailed one man to a tree, where he twitched for a moment before dying.

In the effort to drive the enemy out of the massive buildings, the Marines turned to chemical warfare. Ground launchers lobbed CS tear gas canisters at the enemy, and the choking clouds of drifting gas forced the Marines to wear gas masks. Even Captain Casey's command position in the "rear area" at the MACV Compound was still not safe. Casey recalled that when fixed-wing aircraft were finally able to provide support:

> The first thing they did was drop CS on the north bank. The doggone wind was blowing out of the north back toward the south. We were in the MACV Compound … and we were all wearing gas masks because the CS was all over us. They were firing eight inch artillery from Phu Bai … over to the north (bank), and we were getting huge chunks of shrapnel from that stuff.

Sniper

The practice of remounting the big .50-cal. machine gun on top of the cupola not only made the weapon easier to use, but also solved the problem of limited ammunition supply. When mounted as intended inside the cupola, the cramped space limited the ammunition bin capacity to 50 rounds, but when mounted atop the cupola the ammunition could be linked together in long belts for sustained fire.

Berwick had long accepted the risks he faced by riding exposed atop the turret, but the TCs quickly discovered that the intensity and accuracy of sniper fire in Hue was unlike anything they had previously experienced. Casey said the NVA "got the message early on that as soon as that cupola on that tank opened, they knew a head was coming up. They would have those snipers just zeroed in on that cupola. I lost a couple of TCs and of course this platoon sergeant that way."

The tanks went to the aid of some infantry who were pinned down, and Berwick used the .50-cal. mounted atop the cupola to smash in the windows of buildings on the other side of a wide boulevard. Carlos, now the gunner, was picking his own targets while Berwick hammered away in a sustained sequence of short bursts. Carlos heard the hammering of the machine gun stop and then remain silent. The new loader shouted "Nick's hit!"

Berwick was slumped against the front of the cupola, and his blood was drizzling down into the turret. The loader dragged Berwick down inside as the driver backed the tank into a safe position.

When they had pulled the wounded TC out onto the engine deck a Navy medical corpsman carefully stripped away Berwick's shattered helmet, and tried to assure them that the wound, though serious, might not be life threatening. For the time being Carlos would have to function as both gunner and TC.

Infantrymen dash across the open ground surrounding the traffic circle near the south end of the Nyugen Hoang Bridge. Being too close to a tank could be dangerous in itself, since they tended to attract intense enemy fire. (USMCRC)

New man in town

Tank crew casualties mounted to such a level that men straight off the planes from America were immediately assigned to tank platoons in Hue. Casey said that from the big base at Danang, "They'd fly 'em in by Caribou [the C-7 transport plane] into Phu Bai, and then helicopter them up there."

Parker Butler arrived in Vietnam on February 10, and within 24 hours was aboard a twin-rotor Sea Knight helicopter as it approached the landing zone at the soccer stadium. Parker was helping drag cases of ammunition out of the helicopter when a man in a small truck shouted, "Any eighteen hundreds here?"

When he answered in the affirmative, Parker was taken on a hair-raising ride through the wrecked city. His most lasting impression was the mixed aromas of burned buildings, human excrement, and bodies rotting in the rubble. The blank-faced staff sergeant driving the truck supplied a terse but detailed account of the situation. Not good. The infantry was kicking the NVA out of the heavy stone buildings, but getting mauled in the process. Tank crew losses were heavy.

The truck screeched to a halt behind two tanks, and the driver called out to a round-faced Hispanic tank commander. "New body, Carlos."

"You're my new loader," announced the TC. "Throw your crap on the back and get in. Hurry."

As a new man in-country, Sergeant Butler accepted his new position as loader to a corporal TC, but had little time to think about it. The tank crunched forward through the rubble-filled streets until it reached a broad park-like area devoid of any movement. A rifleman scurried out, grabbed the tank-infantry phone mounted on the back of the tank, and broke in on the crew intercom. He explained that the infantry were pinned down by sniper fire from a tower on the other side of the park.

Parker quickly fell into the routine of feeding the heavy rounds into the big cannon in response to Carlos's commands.

Captain Casey recalled:

One morning there they had a whole infantry platoon pinned down by some NVA that were in a Catholic church, up in the bell tower. They called for a tank to come in there, so we sent a pair of tanks in. They walked mortars right down on top of those tanks but never did get a direct hit on them. We sat there and sent round after round after round into that church, literally destroyed that Catholic church. Finally we silenced that sniper up there, which allowed the infantry to start to move.

The two infantry battalions on the south side were spread through the city. Casey used his two flame tanks "only sparingly" to guard lines of communication between the scattered units.

We probably put out maybe half a dozen rods. A rod is a shot of flame. We were kind of a makeshift company when we went in there. We didn't have the mixer and transfer unit with us. We had a compressor, and what we would do with those aggravating things was load them by hand. We'd pump out of a fifty-five gallon drum of gasoline, five gallons into an old jerry can and pass it up,

M67 flame tanks were externally identical to the M48A3 gun tank. The flame tanks were not as extensively used in Vietnam as they had been in World War II, and in Hue they used their machine guns far more often than the flame projectors. (NARA)

and have a crewman dump it into the tank. Then we'd dump in the thickener [to make the napalm gel].

That night Parker was on watch when the crew of the flame tank spotted figures in the darkness, moving heavy weapons into an isolated building. With a low roar, a tongue of brilliant yellow flame leapt out and swept across the men in the open and into the windows of the building. Parker watched horrified as human torches danced and then exploded as the ammunition they were carrying cooked off. He was even more appalled by the nearby infantry's delighted shouts of "Get some, Zippo!" and the stench that drifted on the wind.

RPG

The next day the tanks were again called up to help the infantry advance down a broad street flanked by large residences. Carlos knew that this was the worst possible situation for his tank. The infantry were fighting their way along as best they could, but could not clear every suicidal enemy from the maze of rooms overlooking the street. Sooner or later their luck would run out.

The tank crept slowly forward, with small-arms fire stinging the exterior. Carlos directed the gunner to engage a machine gun he had spotted in a second-floor window to their right front. As the turret turned, it exposed the thinner armor on the left side to a veteran 18-year-old NVA rocket gunner hidden inside a wrecked house.

Unseen by the tank crew, a single rocket arced out of the building. The slow rockets were visible in flight, and one tanker described them as looking like thrown footballs. It detonated against the side of the turret, just aft of the extra track hung on the sides of the turret to protect it.

Casey said, "When the thing penetrated … when it hits on the inside … the metal from the turret just spalls off. That's where we lost a lot of our crew." The shaped-charge explosion drove through the armor, and a jet of incandescent gas and glowing hot shards of the tank's own armor spewed across the interior to ricochet off the walls and come in contact with the crew. "The ones that took it the hardest when that RPG would penetrate were the gunner and the loader. The TC would get some in the legs every now and then. The driver was safe down there because he's down below that turret, and that shrapnel, as it spalled off in there, wouldn't hit him."

Tanker Terry Hunter described the impact of an RPG as a kind of "slap-boom", followed by a concussion like being hit with a giant hammer. The violence of the explosion could blow a man out of an open hatch.

Parker Butler stepped forward six inches to empty the coaxial machine gun brass bag. The slight movement saved him from being cut in half, but the left side of his body was sprayed with jagged hunks of hot steel. The blast tore through the back of the turret, and other fragments ripped into Carlos's legs.

Numbed by the blast and going into shock, Carlos groaned out "Driver! Back us down. Get into some defilade." The tank lurched backward, crushing the foot of a wounded infantryman who could not scramble out of the path of the blind tank.

The driver negotiated a turn and stopped the tank behind the shelter of a building. The gunner, with only superficial wounds, scrambled past the semi-conscious Carlos and out the hatch. The driver grabbed the limp and bloody Parker by the belt, heaved him up into the loader's hatch opening, and dragged the unconscious man down off the turret and across the engine deck, before passing him down to men waiting on the ground.

As the two men wrestled Carlos out of the commander's cupola and across the engine deck, a medical corpsman attached to an infantry unit frantically cut away Parker's clothing and assessed his wounds. Parker's labored breathing and air bubbles coming out of the wounds indicated punctured lungs. The corpsman's job was not to treat such serious wounds, but to stabilize the victim until he could be transported to more expert medical care. The corpsman quickly wiped away as much blood as possible, and sealed several of the worst wounds with tape and rubber-covered canvas cut from a rain poncho. Other men tied field dressings around Carlos's wounded leg, and the corpsman gave him a morphine injection.

The corpsman supervised as several wounded men were heaved into the back of a truck for a trip to the evacuation point. Shaking one of the less badly wounded to get his full attention, he pointed to Parker. "Make sure he stays on his left side. Otherwise his lungs will fill up with blood." He then slammed his hand on the side of the truck, and waved it away.

Parker Butler, who intended to make a career of the Marine Corps, had lasted thirty-two hours in combat.

As the NVA and VC trapped inside the city were gradually exterminated, the fighting spread to the outskirts of the city, and into the strip of less populous land between the city and the sea. The fighting in and around Hue area lasted until mid-March.

Although losses did not match those among the infantry, casualties among the tank crews were terrible – the highest rate of the war, and all within the space of a single month. The tanks proved tougher than human flesh, and some tanks went through as many as eleven crews as men were wounded, killed, and replaced. Casey said, "Every one of

The RPG-7 (Rocket Propelled Grenade) shoulder-fired rocket launcher was the most common anti-tank weapon used by the NVA and Viet Cong. Older models of RPG were still in use, but the RPG-7 was the most powerful and deadly. (NARA)

those tanks had at least one penetration into the turret, and numerous hits all up and down that tank, from both sides." Decades later he still mourns the loss of a particular staff sergeant, whom he described as the best TC he ever knew. "I had about fifty-five crewmen with those vehicles. I had eleven of the original [men] who came out of there. Fortunately I didn't have that many KIAs. I think I had four KIAs, counting the Staff Sergeant [killed in the river-clearing operation outside the city], and the rest were WIAs."

After the battle

Berwick, Carlos, and Parker were all airlifted to the big hospital at Danang, and eventually to hospitals in the Philippines and the United States. Parker and Carlos made full recoveries, although Parker required lengthy hospitalization. Nick Berwick's head wound impaired his speech, but otherwise left him with his full mental faculties.

Like virtually all Vietnam veterans, all three men went on to build productive lives: Nick supervises land surveying for an energy pipeline corporation; Carlos is a professor at a major university; Parker retired from the Corps in 1986 to pursue his hobby of designing and manufacturing furniture, including a comfortable chair for people with back and thoracic injuries. His factory employs over 200 people.

None of them ever talks about Hue.

BELOW **Tank A-51 belonged to the HQ Platoon, Alpha Company, 1st Tank Battalion, but saw action with 3d Platoon on the north side. The tank, closely protected by infantry, advances alongside the massive walls of The Citadel. (USMCRC)**

RIGHT **A group photo taken by the author at a USMC Vietnam Tankers Association reunion in 2003. Don Gagnon is standing at the far left, Richard "Dick" Carey is seated at the bottom center, John Wear is seated next to the man holding the Marine Corps flag at far right, and Richard Peavey is the man in the hat standing below the flag. Navy Medical Corpsman Gene Hackemack is kneeling at far left. (Author)**

MUSEUMS, COLLECTIONS, AND HISTORICAL RECORDS

The Marine Corps maintains an official Museums and History Branch which operates several facilities. Its resources are essential to anyone conducting serious historical research. At the time this books goes to press (2004) the Branch is in the process of transferring many of its artifacts to a new facility being built by the privately funded Heritage Foundation.

Marine Corps Historical Center
Building 58 of the Washington Naval Yard, Washington, DC, houses the Corps' central archival and museum collections.

Marine Corps Heritage Center, Quantico, Virginia
This museum, scheduled to open in 2004, will become the primary public museum dedicated to the story of the Corps, from 1775 until the present.

Marine Corps Research Center, Quantico, Virginia
This complex, also aboard MCB Quantico, houses an outstanding library, and collections of reports and documents. It is primarily a research and teaching facility for active-duty Marines.

National Archives and Records Administration II
This large facility located in College Park, Maryland, is the permanent custodian of all Marine Corps records, documents, and photographs.

Tank Unit Veterans' Organizations
At this time the primary veterans' organization is the Marine Corps Tankers' Association, headquartered in Oceanside, California. This organization includes veterans from World War II to the Gulf Wars, and holds annual reunions in various parts of the country. It also publishes *MCTA Magazine*, the source of some material for this volume. The subscription contact is: Don Gagnon, Editor, *MCTA Magazine*, 70201 Aurora Road, Number 249, Desert Hot Springs, California, 92241. A separate organization, the USMC Vietnam Tankers' Association, will likely merge with this organization in the future.

Vietnam Veterans' Memorial
Most often called The Wall, this memorial, located on The Mall in Washington, DC, is both staggering and heartbreaking in its simplicity. A walk past The Wall is like a microcosm of the war experience. Enormously controversial when it was first conceived, The Wall has become one of the most visited memorials in the US. The nearby statue of three soldiers, erected as a more conventional memorial at the insistence of those who objected to The Wall, receives less attention.

COLLECTING

At the end of a tour in Vietnam, Marines returned not as units but as groups of individuals. The travel uniform was typically the tan dress uniform, left in storage during the tour of duty. Internet sites such as E-Bay™ are the best potential sources for period items, particularly dress uniforms. However, the collector should be extremely wary of items purportedly used in Vietnam, because as noted, virtually nothing was returned.

Several commercial manufacturers produce accurate replicas of uniforms and some items of equipment. The French magazine *Armes Militaria* is a primary source for both actual artifacts and replicas for the collector.

RE-ENACTMENT

For obvious reasons, re-enactment groups usually consist of people who are safely removed – both in time and space – from the conflict they portray. The Vietnam conflict is still too recent, and controversial, to generate extensive interest in re-enactment. In the United States there are only 12 Vietnam re-enactment groups.

Of course re-enacting the activities of a tank unit is an expensive proposition, complicated by the fact that, to the author's and the Marine

Corps Tanker's Association's knowledge, there are no remaining operable M48A3s. Most groups portray infantry formations, and most of the existing re-enactment groups focus on the various US Army units active in Vietnam.

GLOSSARY

AK-47 – the sturdy Soviet- or Chinese-manufactured Kalashnikov assault rifle, a standard weapon of the VC and NVA.

ARVN – Army of the Republic of Vietnam.

Amtrac – short for amphibian tractor, in Vietnam the box-like LVTP-5.

Blocked – starched and ironed to a regular shape, specifically the proper configuration of the utility cover (hat).

Boonie hat – a generic term for a wide-brimmed sun hat.

Boot – a Marine Corps or Navy recruit trainee.

Bulkhead – a wall. Marines use nautical terminology, including overhead (ceiling), deck (floor), ladderway (stairs), hatch (doorway), and scuttlebutt (drinking fountain).

Cadre – see VC.

Caribou, or C-7 – a twin-engine, short take-off, tactical transport built by DeHavilland Aircraft in Canada.

Chepultepec – a castle on the outskirts of Mexico City, and site of a climactic battle in the Mexican-American War of 1846. It is the "Halls of Montezuma" referred to in the Marine Corps Hymn.

Chow – food; served in a mess or chow hall.

Collar stay – a wire spring used to hold the collar of the uniform dress shirt in place.

Corpsman – a Navy medical corpsman serving with the Marines. Generically called "Doc".

Cover – head cover; any type of soft hat or cap worn by Marines.

Crachin – the cool, ground-hugging fog that forms during the winter monsoon season in Vietnam.

Cupola – the small commander's turret atop the larger main turret of the M48A3 tank.

DI – Drill Instructor.

DMZ – DeMilitarized Zone, the supposedly neutral boundary established as part of the 1953 partition of Vietnam.

Eighteen hundred – verbal shorthand for a person with an 1800-series Military Occupational Specialty; a tank crewman.

Esprit de corps – French "spirit of the corps"; for Marines it refers to the sense of belonging relative to the organisation.

Flak jacket – the armored vest.

Flechette, or beehive round – derives from a term for an arrow. A cannon round that when fired ejected small fin-stabilized metal darts. The darts carried farther and were more stable than the balls in the old canister round. Beehive was derived from the whizzing sound the darts made.

FMF – Fleet Marine Force, specifically the combined arms divisions that are the basis of Marine ground forces. There are three active duty divisions (1st through 3d) and an Active Reserve division (4th Division).

Field scarf – necktie.

GI Bill – a government program dating to the post-World War II era that provided low-interest housing loans, educational stipends, and other assistance to military veterans.

Get Some – to kill or destroy, as in "get some revenge." Also "pop" or "waste".

Gunnery Sergeant, or Gunny – pay grade E-7, a technical rank above Staff Sergeant. The Company Gunny was the senior technical NCO in the unit.

HE – the High Explosive cannon round.

Head – a nautical and Marine Corps term for a latrine; a bathroom or lavatory.

"Hollywood Marine" – a good-natured term for a Marine who attended boot camp at MCRD San Diego.

I Corps ("Eye Corps") – the First Corps operational area; the five northernmost provinces of South Vietnam.

"John Wayne" – after the actor, often used to describe something excessively showy or an overly enthusiastic person. The Confidence Course was sometimes called a "John Wayne Course". A synonym is "gung ho".

KIA – Killed In Action.

LCU – Landing Craft Utility; a Navy coastal craft capable of carrying up to three tanks in an amphibious assault. Used as a coastal and river transport in Vietnam.

LZ – Landing Zone for helicopters. Usually temporary.

Lifer – a career enlisted man.

MACV – Military Assistance Command Vietnam; the multi-service administrative and liaison command responsible for teaching, supplying, and coordinating activities with South Vietnamese units.

MCRD – Marine Corps Recruit Depot; either of the training centers at San Diego, California, or Parris Island, South Carolina.

MOS – Military Occupational Specialty, usually expressed as a number. Infantry was the 0300 series, artillery 0800, and tanks 1800.

Main Force – see VC.

Marine Expeditionary Brigade – a rifle regiment with attached artillery, armor, and logistical support assets. The unit is capable of conducting independent operations.

Master Gunnery Sergeant – pay grade E-9, equivalent to a Sergeant Major. Duties are primarily providing technical leadership rather than administrative duties.

NCO – Non-Commissioned Officer. Marine corps enlisted ranks included non-rated men (Private, Private First Class, and Lance Corporal), NCO (Corporal and Sergeant), and Staff NCO (Staff Sergeant, Gunnery Sergeant, First Sergeant, Master Sergeant, Sergeant Major, and Master Gunnery Sergeant).

NVA – North Vietnamese Army.

OJT – On the Job Training, to learn by doing.

Ontos – Greek for "thing"; the M51 tank destroyer, a small, thinly armored, tracked chassis mounting six 106mm recoilless guns. Originally designed for the Army's airborne formations, it was used in combat only by the Marines.

P-38 – a folding can opener often worn on a neck chain.

PRT – Physical Readiness Test; a timed series of exercises designed to test agility, strength, and endurance.

PX – Post Exchange, a subsidized department store for military personnel.

Pound cake – a dense, high-calorie confection. The name derives from the original recipe (one pound of flour, one pound of milk, one pound of sugar, one pound of eggs, etc.)

RPG – Rocket Propelled Grenade launcher. Any one of a series of Soviet-designed, reusable, shoulder-fired, anti-tank weapons, they combined features of the World War II American "bazooka" and the German *panzerfaust*. Widely used as an anti-tank and anti-personnel weapon by the VC and NVA.

R&R – Rest and Recreation; a temporary leave from the combat zone. Also called I&I for Intoxication and Intercourse, which could also mean Inspector and Instructor.

RVN – Republic of Vietnam.

Sapper – the assault engineers of the VC and NVA, highly skilled in both stealthy assault and combat demolitions.

Seabag – a canvas duffel bag used to ship and store personal property and uniforms; the Marine's "luggage".

Semper Fi – from the Marine Corps motto, *Semper Fidelis*. An all-purpose exclamation, the meaning depends upon context, from "greetings" to "tough luck".

Shit detail – a generic term for any type of unpleasant duty, from cleaning the heads to a dangerous task in combat.

Shitfister – a tracked vehicle mechanic.

Short, or Short-timer – a man nearing the end of his tour of duty in Vietnam.

Skivvies – the generic term for underwear, reportedly derived from the Japanese word for a rice-paper condom.

Snuffy – a new man; a term used only by Marine Corps tankers. The origin is unknown, but was probably derived from the old Snuffy Smith comic strip.

Spalling – when fragments of the tank's own armor are blown off the interior surfaces, making deadly high-speed shrapnel.

TC – Tank Commander.

Utilities or utility uniform – the combination work/combat uniform first issued in World War II. Several models were used over the course of the Vietnam War.

VC or Viet Cong – a derivative of the term for a Vietnamese Communist; the combat arms of the VC were divided into Local Cadres (part-time local guerrillas) and Main Force (permanent standing units). Also called Victor Charlie, Mister Charles, or more rarely Nguyen.

WIA – Wounded In Action.

WP or Willy Peter – the White Phosphorus Smoke round, also used to attack personnel. Can also refer to Water Proof.

Warrant Officer – intermediate ranks between Staff NCO and commissioned officer, usually awarded in recognition of technical expertise. Often addressed as "Gunner" from the rank of Gun Captain in the old battleship Navy.

World, The – The United States; anywhere except the Vietnam combat zone.

Zippo – M67 flame tank, nicknamed after a reliable brand of cigarette lighter. This vehicle was unique to the Marines.

BIBLIOGRAPHY

Very little generally available literature deals specifically or even in passing with Marine Corps tank operations in Vietnam. Several of the following are more general references on the Marine Corps' role in the conflict, or on the specific actions described in this volume.

Anonymous, "Ambush at Con Thien", in *Newsweek Magazine*, July 17, 1967, pp. 45–46.

Carey, Richard D., "dev-as-tate: de- + vasatare: 'to lay waste'", in *Marine Corps Tanker's Association Magazine*, June 1999, p. 6.

Coan, Jim, *Con Thien: The Hill of Angels*, University of Alabama Press, Tuscaloosa AL, 2004. A junior tank officer's first-person account of the bitter battles against the powerful NVA forces deployed along the DMZ.

Estes, Kenneth W., *Marines Under Armor: The Marine Corps and the Armored Fighting Vehicle, 1916–2000*, Naval Institute Press, Annapolis MD, 2000. An overview of the history of USMC armored doctrine.

Headquarters, Department of the Army, *Operator's Manual, Tank, Combat, Full Tracked: 90-mm Gun, M48A3 W/E (2350-895-9154) TM 9-2350-224-10*, Washington, DC, 1966.

Millett, Allen R., *Semper Fidelis: The History of the United States Marine Corps*, Macmillan Publishing, New York and Collier Macmillan Publishing, London, 1980. An excellent overview of the complexities – both military and political – of the war.

Murphy, Edward F., *Semper Fi Vietnam*, Presidio, Novato, California, 1997. A chronological overview of USMC combat actions in Vietnam.

Nalty, Bernard C., *The Vietnam War*, Salamander Books, New York, 1998.

Nolan, Keith William, *Battle for Hue: Tet 1968*, Presidio, Novato, California, 1983. Perhaps the best overview of the battle for Hue.

NON-RATED			NCO		STAFF NCO			
NO BADGE							FIRST SERGEANT	SERGEANT MAJOR
PRIVATE	PRIVATE FIRST CLASS	LANCE CORPORAL	CORPORAL	SERGEANT	STAFF SERGEANT	GUNNERY SERGEANT	MASTER SERGEANT	MASTER GUNNERY SERGEANT

U S MARINE CORPS ENLISTED RANKS

ABOVE **Marine Corps officer ranks were identical to those of the Army, but enlisted ranks did not include the "Specialist" ratings. First Sergeants and Sergeant Majors performed primarily administrative duties, while Master Sergeants and Master Gunnery Sergeants were high-level technical specialists. (After "Handbook for Marines", 1967 edition)**

RIGHT **Vietnamese civilians were both spectators and victims when the fighting swept over their villages. These children are watching tanks and infantry outside a small village in the coastal area and Viet Cong stronghold south of Marble Mountain. (NARA)**

Peavey, Robert E., "Turning the Table on Mr. Charles", in *Marine Corps Tanker's Association Magazine*, March 2000, pp. 10–12.

Peavey, Robert E., "Scratch My Back", *Marine Corps Tanker's Association Magazine*, December 2000, pp. 12 – 14.

Starry, Donn A., *Armored Combat In Vietnam*, Arno Press, New York, 1980. Deals primarily with US Army experiences, and only peripherally with USMC tank actions.

Warr, Nicholas, *Phase Line Green: the Battle for Hue, 1968*, Ivy Books, New York, 1997. A junior infantry officer's memoir of the battle.

Wear, John, "Two Days in Hue City, Tet 1968", *Marine Corps Tanker's Association Magazine*, March 2000, pp. 8–9.

COLOR PLATE COMMENTARY

PLATE A. BASIC CREWMAN UNIFORMS AND MAINTENANCE EQUIPMENT, 1967–68

This tanker in training at Camp Pendleton, California is wearing the M62 pattern utility uniform and heavy leather boots that were the standard uniform in the period 1967–68. This Marine is dusty and rumpled after a day in the semi-arid training areas along the southern California coast. His sleeves are rolled above the elbow in deference to the heat; there was no short sleeve uniform jacket. Each morning the trainee would change into a newly laundered and ironed uniform, and boots would be freshly polished each night. The rank badges indicate a Private First Class, a typical rank at this stage of the young Marine's service. In his right hand he holds the heavy pinch bar used to move heavy objects and to test the tension of the tank track. With his left hand he supports the massive 3.155in. wrench used to make fine adjustments to the track tension by turning a large nut, moving the tension adjustment idler (the most forward wheel of the tank) forward or backward. Improper tension could cause the track to slip off the wheels in a turn, disabling the vehicle. **1.** Detail of the iron-on transfer used to mark the left breast pocket of the jacket to distinguish the wearer from members of other services. There were slight variations of font, and of the size of the Corps symbol relative to the letters. Because of the limitations of the manufacturing process for the iron-on transfers, the symbol did not exhibit the fine detail of modern iron-on transfers. The name was stamped above the pocket using a rubber frame with letters that could be inserted to make up the name, purchased as part of the recruit's PX supplies. The ink of both the transfer and the stamp tended to bleed or blur on the cloth, and disappeared with repeated launderings. **2.** An alternative type of jacket, much less common, had concealed buttons, and a large internal map pocket inside the left side of the jacket. **3.** The inside of the jacket, showing the large map pocket. The pocket was held closed by a single button. **4.** The canvas seabag was the individual's primary article of luggage, and packing all the uniforms and other belongings inside required considerable organizational skill. Seabags were typically marked with the individual's name and usually some distinctive pattern applied with a felt-tip pen or paint in order to identify it in a large pile of similar baggage when the unit moved. It was locked with a combination lock or padlock through the metal clip that secured the top opening. **5.** These three items were used as an assembly when installing or removing the large bolts that held the track components together. They are **(a)** the T-sliding wrench drive, **(b)** the extension, and **(c)** a wrench socket. The tank carried a comprehensive toolkit, but these items were among the most commonly used. In addition, crews sometimes carried a length of iron pipe that could be slipped over the T-drive to provide additional leverage. **6.** The TM 9-2350-224-10 training manual for the M48A3 tank was a comprehensive operating guide to the tank, all its ancillary equipment, and common maintenance procedures. It was bound together by three aluminum screws so that pages could be removed or inserted as the manual was updated. A copy of the manual was part of the tank's equipment. **7.** Detail of standard web belt for trousers, with brass buckle and tip. The Corps used an open-frame buckle unlike the rectangular plate of the Army pattern belt. The open frame buckle had an interior lock, such that when secured only the rectangular frame showed. The metal parts were brass and kept polished to a high shine, including the interior parts that were not normally visible. **8.** The heavy wool-blend, cushion-sole socks had a thin upper part, thicker on the foot segment, and with additional padding on the sole. The heavy socks were designed to wick moisture from inside the boot, and to pad the foot to keep it from slipping inside the boot, a common cause of friction blisters. **9.** The heavy combat boots were made of thick black leather with aluminum lacing eyelets and a thick composition rubber sole held on by stitching and brass tacks. Individuals could, at their own expense, have the eyelets replaced by hooks for "speed lacing". These sturdy boots provided good protection when working with heavy machinery, but were unsuited to the climate of Vietnam. **10.** Rank badges were worn on the collar of the jacket, and occasionally on the front of the utility cover. The devices were made of black-enameled metal, held on by pins that went through the fabric and were secured by brass clasps on the underside. The two rank badges shown are for a Corporal (two stripes and crossed rifles) and a Sergeant (three stripes and crossed rifles). The infantry frequently did not wear rank devices in the field, but tankers – less vulnerable to having leaders singled out by snipers – commonly wore the badges in combat. **11.** Identity disks or dog tags were commonly worn around the neck. The identity tag is stamped aluminum, and reads in the format: family name – GILBERT; individual name: – O. E. JR.; service number – 2440668; blood type – O (a negative blood type would have been stamped O-); branch of service – USMC; gas mask size – M; and religion – BAPTIST. The seven-digit service number was still in use in the early days of the Vietnam War, before it was replaced by the nine-digit Social Security Number used today. The other item is a folding P-38 can opener, used to open canned rations. It is made of dark gray steel with a lighter colored anodized coating that quickly wore away. Both were commonly worn on a breakaway aluminum chain of the type commonly used as key chains. It was also common to wear one of the two dog tags attached to the bootlaces to facilitate identification if the body was dismembered. **12.** A plastic gooseneck flashlight, with a set of colored plastic filters carried inside the battery compartment cap, was part of the tank's kit. The tank driver's visibility was very poor, and a foot guide commonly used the light to direct the tank in darkness. **13.** The utility cover was another uniquely Marine Corps item of clothing, distinct from the cylindrical and later baseball-style caps worn by the Army. Several designs of utility cover differed only in the details of the stitching. All designs had the two small ventilation grommets on either side. **14.** The tanker's crash helmet had built-in earphones and an adjustable boom-mounted microphone connected to the tank's intercom and radio system.

PLATE B. PUGIL STICK DRILL, LATE STAGE OF RECRUIT TRAINING

Training with pugil sticks was intended to simulate hand-to-hand combat with the clubbed rifle and bayonet, but more importantly, it instilled an aggressive and combative attitude in the recruit. This type of training was usually conducted as a competition between sub-units, most commonly between squads within a training platoon. Mock battles might be one-on-one (most common), two-on-one or even three-on-one. Protective gear included a football helmet and face mask, heavily padded gauntlets or ice hockey gloves, and a crotch protector that slipped over the trousers. All of these items were locally made or purchased at local sporting goods stores, and varied widely in design and workmanship. The recruits formed a circle to observe and cheer, boo, or shout advice as at a sporting match. Recruits were taught specific blows and parries, but in the heat of combat often just flailed away at each other until the Drill Instructor referee declared a winner. In this match the man on the right is making an inefficient blocking motion rather than a proper parry. The recruit on the left is about to connect with a vertical butt stroke similar to a boxer's uppercut, one of the standard killing blows delivered to the opponent's groin, torso, or face with the butt of the rifle. Drill Instructors remained almost supernaturally neat at all times. In order to maintain the illusion that they did not sweat or get dirty, they changed uniforms as many as four times daily. Recruits wore no rank badges as all were privates. A Drill Instructor typically held the rank of Sergeant, Staff Sergeant, or Gunnery Sergeant, although a select few were Corporals. The Drill Instructor is wearing the distinctive "Smoky Bear" campaign hat worn only by Drill Instructors and Marksmanship Instructors, and a polished black leather sword belt indicating his position as the Senior Drill Instructor of a three-man team.

PLATE C. VEHICLE MAINTENANCE AND REPAIR EQUIPMENT

This plate depicts a few of the more important items out of the hundreds necessary to keep the tank in operation. Maintenance was performed on a rigorous schedule, with some items checked on a daily or weekly basis, some on intervals determined by the number of hours the tank was in operation (based on readings from a cumulative clock inside the turret), while other items were literally checked each time the tank came to a halt. Maintenance steps and repairs as well as operational hours were recorded in the Tank Commander's logbook, a loose-leaf binder kept with the tank. The items are grouped according to function: items relating to the tank's main gun are at the top, some general and track maintenance items below, and important hand tools at the bottom. **1.** The five Shaft Sections were used for cleaning the main gun bore, or removing jammed or misfired rounds. These were made of either wood painted dark green, with matt-finish cast aluminum fittings on either end, or all-aluminum rods. **2.** The Bore Brush consisted of stiff brass wire bristles mounted on a steel ring that fitted over the bore brush assembly. **3.** The Bore Brush Assembly fitted onto the end of the staff sections, and carried the bore brush. **4.** The bore brush and the bore brush assembly were stored in the Bore Brush Cover, a canvas bag with drawstring closure. **5.** The Chain Hoist hooked to the interior roof of the turret, and was used to suspend the weight of the massive breechblock assembly when performing maintenance on the main gun. **6.** The Muzzle Cover was another canvas bag with snap closures, used to keep water and foreign matter out of the main gun bore during storage or shipment. **7.** The Ramming Tool Extractor was used to extract brass casings that did not properly eject after firing, or misfired rounds. It hooked onto the rim of the shell casing, and the loader pried the empty casing out of the chamber. **8.** The Loader used the Asbestos Mitt to handle hot shell casings from the main gun, and to change overheated machine-gun barrels. **9.** The Vehicle Logbook was used to record all repairs, maintenance, damage, and system malfunctions, as well as to record the number of operating hours in order to determine major maintenance intervals. **10.** Fuel Cans were carried as spares to facilitate refueling by hand if necessary. **11.** The Flexible Spout screwed into the mouth of the fuel can to reduce spillage. **12.** The First Aid Kit was carried inside the turret, and contained basic medical supplies and field dressings for wounds. **13.** The Stove Can held a small gasoline-fueled Coleman™ cooking stove, a simple aluminum cylinder sealed with tape. **14.** Three cloth Signal Flags – green, orange, and red – were used primarily as range safety markers, or to indicate a broken-down vehicle. The pockets sewn along one side of the flag fitted over a wooden flagstaff. **15.** The Flagstaffs were simple wooden dowels. **16.** The Signal Flag Case was used to store the flags and staffs. **17.** Two Track Tools with handles were carried by each tank, and were one of the most important repair items. The jaws at each end hooked over the two ends of a broken track, and the screw drive pulled the ends back together. **18.** The Mechanical Puller was used to install and remove the bolts that held the track end connectors that linked each of the individual track links. **19.** Each tank carried a number of spare End

Maintenance gear for an M48A3 tank, laid out for inspection. Most of these items are illustrated in the Plates. The coiled items at upper left are the refueling hoses and hand pump, and the slave cable used to start a tank with dead batteries. (NARA)

Connectors. These parts of the track were the most vulnerable to breakage, and were checked at each halt. **20.** The Spent Shell Bag for the coaxial machine gun clipped onto the side of the weapon and collected the spent brass and belt links to keep them from fouling the interior of the turret. Emptying this bag was one of the Loader's primary tasks. **21.** Five Brass Padlocks with keys were provided to secure the external stowage boxes and the hatches. **22.** The Grease Gun and its Extensions was one of the tools most important to the tank, used to inject grease under pressure into special nipple fittings called "zerts". Wheel bearings were greased at frequent intervals to avoid failure. **23.** The Hand Oiler was used to apply lightweight liquid lubricants to mechanical and weapons parts. **24.** Wire Cutters were commonly used to cut away communications wire or barbed wire that had fouled the track or wheels. **25.** Tank crewmen were frequently required to make hasty repairs in the field, and a variety of Files could be used to modify or reshape damaged parts. **26** and **27.** A Cold Chisel and Ballpeen Hammer were used to cut away wire that had become too tightly wrapped around a wheel or axle to cut with the wire cutters, or to remove damaged and fused parts. **28.** The tool kit included a variety of Screwdrivers, including this big 15 in. (38cm) tool. **29.** The Lubrication Orders were printed sheets used as visual reminders of the dozens of moving parts that had to be lubricated each day. **30.** The tool kit also included a large assortment of wrenches, such as this large Adjustable Crescent Wrench.

PLATE D. COMBAT TACTICS AND ACTION, SOUTH OF MARBLE MOUNTAIN

The primary purpose of Marine Corps tanks in the Vietnam War was to provide mobile firepower for the infantry. Individual platoons of five tanks, or sections of two or three tanks, were typically attached to infantry units. In offensive actions the tanks frequently functioned as assault guns, and as such were controlled by the infantry unit commander. Here a Viet Cong prisoner – crouching at right center – has guided the Marines to a bunker hidden behind the small knoll at left. The plate illustrates typical *ad hoc* tactics. The tank commander is standing exposed in his cupola so that he can better spot the target in the dense plant growth. An infantryman crouches in the protection offered by the turret, and helps the tank commander to spot and direct the cannon fire. One Marine infantryman guards the prisoner, while others wait in various postures of readiness to assault

the position once the tank has done its work. The area beyond the tank is partially obscured by very light gray smoke from the cannon, and by dust raised by the muzzle blast. The tank commander is partially obscured by a cloud of white smoke coming out of the loader's hatch. When the main gun fired and the breech opened, a cloud of smoke and acidic gas from partially burned propellant would often flow back into the turret, so the crews typically operated with the turret hatches open. The very light-colored sandy soil was typical of the ancient beach dunes that underlay much of the coastal I Corps area where the Marines operated. This plate is based on photographs of 1st Battalion tanks operating in support of Marine Infantrymen south of Marble Mountain.

PLATE E. DAILY LIFE – TANK TRACK REPAIR

The one constant in a tanker's life in Vietnam was the continuous and unremitting requirement for vehicle maintenance and repair. Here three tank crewmen work to repair a track broken by a mine south of Marble Mountain. The two standing men are using pinch bars to lever up the "live" track to relieve tension so that the kneeling man can tighten the guide tooth bolts. The various tools are shown in Plate A. In the background is an LVTP-5 amtrac, often used as a personnel carrier on land though it was ill suited to the task. Prolonged driving on land damaged the small road wheels of the LVTP-5, necessitating constant and difficult repairs. The fuel cells for the gasoline engine were built into the floor of the amtrac, making it extremely vulnerable to mines, and the infantry often chose to ride on top, rather than risk incineration inside if the vehicle struck a mine. The large drum tied to the top of the vehicle contained drinking water. The front of the amtrac is to the left; the box-like design made it difficult to tell front from rear when viewed from a distance.

PLATE F. URBAN COMBAT, TET OFFENSIVE, 1968

The urban combat required to recapture of the old Imperial City of Hue in early 1968 was some of the most intense of the Vietnam War, and tanks played a larger role than was typical of Vietnam combat. The number of tanks was small, but they provided precise firepower in assaults on heavy masonry buildings, and drew enemy fire away from the infantry. The tanks, and particularly the crews, paid a heavy price. The enemy's anti-tank RPG rockets would not usually destroy or even seriously damage the vehicle itself, but penetrations were often devastating to the crew. Numerous crewmen were killed or wounded, and most tanks survived four or more complete crews. One measure to provide increased protection against these rockets was to hang extra track blocks from the turret rails, visible in many period photos. This tank is fighting its way up one of the broad streets on the south side of the Perfume River. One factor that contributed to the nightmarish

The huge M51 retriever was built on the chassis of the M103 heavy tank, and these vehicles operated right up front with the tanks. Tank repairmen were awarded two of the Navy Crosses awarded to tank battalion personnel. (NARA)

Unit One Field Surgical Kit over one shoulder, and used empty rifle ammunition bandoliers to carry additional battle dressings. The front-line corpsman's job was simply to provide sufficient care to prevent immediate death, and to stabilize the patient for transport to a field surgical hospital. In order to function under extreme stress, in the confusion of combat, and under immediate threat of fire or explosion, tank crews learned a standard drill to evacuate wounded crew members. The turret hatches provided the largest openings for evacuation of incapacitated men, even drivers. The usual procedure was to move the tank to a covered position, if possible, and turn the turret in such a way as to place the bulk of the turret and armored frontal surfaces between the rescue party and potential enemy fire. Usually one man would lift the casualty from inside the turret by holding him around the chest, while a man outside pulled him out by grasping his clothing, or in some cases a sling improvised from a belt. The rescuer would then drag the wounded man off of the turret and into the shelter of the turret on the engine deck, and toward the rear of the tank. Wounded were moved to the ground by pulling them head first off the deck, supporting the head and shoulders, then a second man (if available) would grasp the legs and lower them to the ground. In this scene the corpsman has used his heavy fighting knife to cut away Parker's clothing and assess his wounds, while other crewmen and nearby infantrymen help drag the less severely wounded Carlos from the tank.

PLATE H. BASIC CREWMAN UNIFORM AND EQUIPMENT, REPUBLIC OF VIETNAM

This figure is a typical tank crewman in Vietnam, attired in jungle utilities, jungle boots, and a floppy "boonie hat". The trouser legs are rolled into loose cuffs above the ankle, rather than bloused around the boot tops. He is holding one of the M71 High Explosive (HE) rounds for the 90mm main gun; this was the type of ammunition most commonly used. There were several fuzes for this round, and this illustration shows the M51A5 impact-detonated fuze. **1.** The M51 Armored Vest was not worn inside the tank because of its bulk, but was kept close at hand for wear outside the tank. The tank commander wore his vest more than any other crewman because he frequently rode exposed atop the turret. **2.** The M336 Canister round fired a thin metal container filled with 1,281 spherical steel pellets. Air resistance caused the thin metal covering to peel away, releasing the pellets in a cloud like a gigantic shotgun blast. **3.** The M318A1 Armor-Piercing Tracer (AP-T) round was a solid metal shot used to attack armored vehicles. It incorporated a chemical tracer in the base of the projectile, which allowed the gunner and tank commander to follow the flight path of the projectile. This round was seldom used in Vietnam. **4.** The M431E1 High-Explosive Anti-Tank (HEAT) round fired a shaped-charge projectile. Upon impact the explosion formed a focused jet of incandescent gas that could burn through armor. The long probe at the front was the detonator, which insured that the round detonated at the proper "stand-off distance" to provide maximum focus for the penetrating jet. **5.** The M313 and similar M313C Smoke (WP)

battle in southern Hue was the construction of the buildings. Buildings on the south (new city) side of the Perfume River were French colonial in design, and constructed of sturdy brick or concrete, coated with decorative stucco. Most buildings were enclosed within low masonry walls or decorative fences of black-painted iron, and walled back gardens turned each residential block into a compartmentalized fortress. The Chinese-manufactured RPG rockets were slow in flight, and were sometimes mistaken for birds. A significant tactical drawback was that the rocket left a faint light ocher-colored smoke trail that gave away the position of the firer. In the random chance that often determined life or death in battle, the tank in this plate has rotated its turret and inadvertently exposed the weaker armor of the turret side to a rocket gunner hidden in a building. The shaped-charge warhead has just detonated against the turret with a bright flash.

PLATE G. AFTER BATTLE – IMMEDIATE MEDICAL ATTENTION AND FIRST AID

Marines considered themselves an elite, and often looked down upon members of the other services. No one, though, was more highly regarded by Marines than the Navy "Docs", the medical corpsmen attached to each unit. These men frequently risked – and sometimes sacrificed – their own lives to rescue and treat Marines wounded on the battlefield. Although a tank battalion in Vietnam had its own medical staff, in combat immediate services were more likely provided by whichever corpsman was closest to hand, usually one belonging to an infantry unit. Corpsmen normally carried basic surgical instruments and medications in the cartridges were filled with white phosphorus (usually called WP or "Willie Peter") and an explosive bursting charge. On exposure to air, the phosphorus burst into flame. The round was used to create smokescreens, mark targets for artillery or air attack, and to inflict casualties. The burning phosphorus would cling tenaciously to clothing and flesh. The designers provided the 90mm tank gun with an astonishing variety of specialized ammunition. Some other types of rounds not shown here included Armor Piercing Capped with Tracer (APC-T), Hypervelocity Armor Piercing with Tracer (HVAP-T), High Explosive with Tracer (HE-T), High Explosive Plastic with Tracer (HEP-T; equivalent to the British High-Explosive Squash Head, or HESH, round), Target Practice (TP), Target Practice with Tracer (TP-T), Hypervelocity Target Practice with Tracer (HVTP-T), and dummy or inert rounds used to practice loading drill. **6.** The .50-cal. M2HB machine gun mounted in the cupola required special kit modification for proper function inside the small space. The modifications included a chain-activated charging handle to operate the bolt and chamber rounds, an electrical firing solenoid system to replace the "butterfly" trigger on the rear of the weapon, and a flexible chute and collecting bag for used brass. Barrels were interchangeable, but this was not actually practical with the cupola mounting. **7.** The M2HB could fire several types of round; shown here are ball (the copper-jacketed lead round used against personnel or vehicles), tracer (orange tipped), armor piercing (black tipped), and incendiary (blue tipped). Not shown are armor-piercing incendiary (tipped in aluminum or blue with an aluminum band), armor-piercing incendiary tracer (red tipped with an aluminum band), blanks, and dummy rounds (with perforated casings). **8.** The M3A1 "Grease Gun" submachine gun fired the same .45-cal. round as the M1911 pistol and the Thompson submachine gun. Designed during World War II specifically as a weapon for tank crewmen, its primary virtue was low cost. The bolt cover is shown open to depict the two tapered holes in the bolt assembly; the user chambered a round and armed the firing mechanism by inserting a finger into the forward hole, drawing the bolt back, and releasing it. Although the round was deadly, the weapon was extremely inaccurate, easily damaged, and often unreliable. Most tank crewmen relied on pistols and either M14 or M16 rifles for close defense. **9.** Jungle boots came in several patterns with various identifying features. These early pattern boots have brass screen drains in the insteps, and a simple design for the leather heel cap. **10.** The powerful .45-cal. M1911A1 pistol was designed in 1908, and remained the standard American military sidearm for decades. Although difficult to fire accurately because of the heavy weight and powerful recoil, British weapons expert Ian Hogg's observation that "impact of over 300 foot pounds (of impact energy) on any part of the body guaranteed disablement" was an accurate assessment of the reason for its popularity. The detachable magazine held seven rounds. **11.** The pistol was normally carried in a brown leather holster on the belt, but tank crews were issued a black leather shoulder holster. **12.** The bulky kidney plates in the back of the armored vests worn by the Marines were their most distinctive feature. It was common to apply the name to the back of the vest, and when one man left and another inherited the vest, he simply painted over the old name and added his own. Markings were applied with whatever color of paint was available. Personal graffiti were also commonly seen on these vests. **13.** The tank's tow cables were much shorter than commonly perceived. The cable was braided steel, and was kept greased and oiled, but usually showed some signs of rust.

The US Navy provided chaplains for the Marine Corps. Chaplains served all Marines regardless of religious denomination. This chaplain is conducting Roman Catholic Christmas Mass with a stack of ration boxes as a makeshift altar. (USMCRC)

INDEX

Figures in **bold** refer to illustrations.

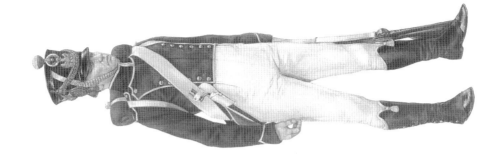

OSPREY
PUBLISHING

FIND OUT MORE ABOUT OSPREY

❏ Please send me the latest listing of Osprey's publications

❏ I would like to subscribe to Osprey's e-mail newsletter

Title / rank

Name

Address

City / county

Postcode / zip   state / country

e-mail

WAR

I am interested in:

❏ Ancient world
❏ Medieval world
❏ 16th century
❏ 17th century
❏ 18th century
❏ Napoleonic
❏ 19th century

❏ American Civil War
❏ World War 1
❏ World War 2
❏ Modern warfare
❏ Military aviation
❏ Naval warfare

Please send to:

USA & Canada:
Osprey Direct USA, c/o MBI Publishing, P.O. Box 1,
729 Prospect Avenue, Osceola, WI 54020

UK, Europe and rest of world:
Osprey Direct UK, P.O. Box 140, Wellingborough,
Northants, NN8 2FA, United Kingdom

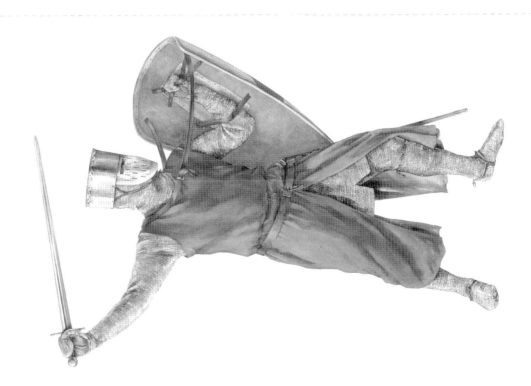

OSPREY
PUBLISHING

www.ospreypublishing.com

call our telephone hotline
for a free information pack

USA & Canada: 1-800-826-6600
UK, Europe and rest of world call:
+44 (0) 1933 443 863

Young Guardsman
Figure taken from *Warrior 22:
Imperial Guardsman 1799–1815*
Published by Osprey
Illustrated by Richard Hook

Knight, c.1190
Figure taken from *Warrior 1: Norman Knight 950 – 1204 AD*
Published by Osprey
Illustrated by Christa Hook

POSTCARD